Competency Based Teacher Education: Professionalizing Social Studies Teaching

Dell Felder, Editor

Bulletin 56

 NATIONAL COUNCIL FOR THE SOCIAL STUDIES

NATIONAL COUNCIL FOR THE SOCIAL STUDIES

President
Anna S. Ochoa
Indiana University
Bloomington, Indiana

President-Elect
George G. Watson, Jr.
Winchester High School
Winchester, Massachusetts

Vice-President
Todd Clark
Constitutional Rights
  Foundation
Los Angeles, California

Executive Director
Brian J. Larkin
Washington, D.C.

Editor
Daniel Roselle
Washington, D.C.

Executive Secretary Emeritus
Merrill F. Hartshorn
Washington, D.C.

Directors
Daniel L. Austin
Marilyn Moody Garavaglia
June V. Gilliard
Carole Hahn
Savannah Jones
Jack Linden
Wilma Lund
Howard D. Mehlinger
Richard F. Newton
Geraldine Rosenthal
Arthur L. Thesenvitz
Richard Simms, *Ex Officio*

Publications Board
Gaylord C. Lasher, *Chairperson*
Charles L. Mitsakos, *Coordinator and Past-Chairperson*
Geneva Gay
June Gould
Carole Hahn
Karen B. Wiley
Elmer Williams
Todd Clark, *Ex Officio*
Fay D. Metcalf, *Ex Officio*

Library of Congress Catalog Card Number: 78-58629
ISBN 0-87986-020-0
Copyright © 1978 by the
NATIONAL COUNCIL FOR THE SOCIAL STUDIES
2030 M Street, N.W., Washington, D.C. 20036

Foreword

Particularly in the field of social studies, competency based teacher education is a controversial concept. Once entered into a dialogue, it divides teacher education into distinct camps. Some find it antithetical to the humanistic goals of social studies. Others see it as a way of bringing clarity and precision to a disorderly and soft profession. Still others try to synthesize different points of view, using a CBTE model for achieving some of their goals and not using it for others.

How to prepare social studies teachers effectively is a question that remains unanswered. We have difficulty defining and even more difficulty agreeing on the characteristics, attitudes, or behaviors of an effective teacher. However controversial, CBTE offers one systematic response. In effect, CBTE has breathed some fire and life into teacher education over the last decade. Ten years of CBTE notwithstanding, only scanty reference to it has been made in the social studies literature. We have, for the most part, ignored it as a field. Under the CBTE rubric there have been substantial development, implementation, and research efforts. At its maximum, the movement has identified specific outcomes and programs for preparing teachers; at a minimum, it has provided a point of departure or a position against which to react.

This bulletin not only describes CBTE, but it also explains its particular relationship to the social studies. Further, it speaks to a long-time criticism of CBTE. It has often been charged that CBTE can deal with low-level cognitive learnings, but not with higher-level affective ones. Two chapters in this bulletin are devoted to affective teaching competencies and multicultural education.

Dell Felder appropriately describes teaching as an emergent profession. Reluctantly, most of us would have to agree. She predicates this well conceptualized bulletin on the assumption that CBTE is a vehicle for professionalizing teaching. It is important to read this book from that perspective.

This bulletin will please some and anger others. Undoubtedly, it will elicit both supportive and critical response. Regardless of one's point of view, the bulletin makes an important contribution to the teacher education literature—particularly in social studies. NCSS owes a deep debt of gratitude to editor Dell Felder and to her highly qualified authors for their thoughtful and thorough work in our behalf.

Anna S. Ochoa, *President*
National Council for the Social Studies

About the Editor

Dell Felder is Associate Dean for Graduate Studies and Professor of Curriculum and Instruction in the College of Education at the University of Houston, Texas. She is also Director of that institution's competency based undergraduate teacher education program. Author, curriculum designer, and consultant, she has provided leadership in the development of educational programs in various states of the nation, and has served as Visiting Professor at the Universidad Autonoma de Guadalajara, and at Levinsky College, Israel.

Chapter Authors

Geneva Gay, Associate Professor of Education,
Purdue University

Jane McCarthy Goldstein, Teaching Assistant,
Curriculum and Instruction Department,
College of Education, University of Houston

Thomas W. Hewitt, Assistant Professor of
Curriculum and Instruction, College of Education,
Kansas State University

Loye Y. Hollis, Professor of Curriculum and Instruction
and Associate Dean for Undergraduate Studies,
College of Education, University of Houston

Robert B. Howsam, Professor of Educational Administration
and Dean, College of Education,
University of Houston

John Jarolimek, Professor of Education,
University of Washington

Carl E. Schomburg, Professor of Curriculum and Instruction,
College of Education, University of Houston

Wilford A. Weber, Professor of Curriculum and Instruction,
College of Education, University of Houston

Contents

Foreword   iii
   Anna S. Ochoa

Introduction   vi
   Dell Felder

Part One: Professionalizing Social Studies Teaching   1
1. Challenges in Professionalizing
   Social Studies Teaching   3
   Robert B. Howsam

2. The Basics in Social Studies:
   Implications for the Preparation of Teachers   17
   John Jarolimek

Part Two: CBTE: Definition and Example   39
3. Competency Based Teacher Education:
   Past, Present and Future   40
   Loye Y. Hollis

4. Integrating the Social Studies Component
   in a CBTE Model   58
   Carl E. Schomburg

Part Three: Issues and Opportunities   71
5. Affective Teaching Competencies
   and Competency Based Teacher Education   73
   Wilford A. Weber and Jane McCarthy Goldstein

6. Interfacing CBTE and Multicultural Education
   in Social Studies Teacher Preparaton   85
   Geneva Gay

7. Competency-Referenced Professional Development   102
   Thomas W. Hewitt

Index   115

Introduction

Dell Felder

Competency based teacher education was initially conceptualized as a means for moving teaching toward its professional destiny. The movement has been in existence for ten years. During that time attention has been focused primarily on defining, developing, and testing CBTE as an instructional approach for the preparation of teachers. Attention to development has tended to obscure the originally conceived purpose of CBTE. This volume will return to that original intent and will view CBTE from the perspective of professionalizing teaching.

Teaching is not yet a profession. It does not yet possess all of the characteristics or meet all of the standards associated with professional status. Chief among the professional deficits which CBTE can best address are:

- teaching does not yet possess a body of knowledge and a repertoire of behaviors which are universally accepted as associated with the practice of teaching;
- teaching has not yet established agreed upon standards for admission to and continuance within the profession.

There are those who doubtless would argue the validity of the above assertions. They could point to numerous examples of knowledge and skills assumed to be associated with teaching. They could argue that certification standards are enforced nationwide as conditions for entry into the profession. Closer examination, however, would yield little empirically validated knowledge as a base for the practice of teaching or the preparation of teachers. Given this void, neither the public nor the profession can place high confidence in certification standards as a means for assuring that those who enter teaching are qualified to discharge its responsibilities. Furthermore, the right to certify those who teach does not belong to the teaching profession; it belongs to the state. Teaching, as a collective body of practitioners, and teachers, as individual professionals, have not yet been recognized and sanctioned by society as fully professional.

It is not easy for most teachers to accept the notion that theirs is a semi-professional status. In most cases they have received the best training available. In almost all cases they are dedicated and committed to what they are doing. They generally perceive their services to students as of equal (if not greater) importance than the services provided by the more established professions.

Growing numbers of teachers, however, are becoming aware of the importance of recognizing the current status of teaching for what it is. Teaching is an *emergent profession* destined, many hope, to achieve full professional status in just a matter of time. Emergent professions by definition are dynamically developing, moving closer and closer to meeting the standards established and accepted by society as characteristic of fully mature professions. More and more teachers are urging that the efforts of teacher education and the organized teaching profession be directed toward the relentless pursuit of those standards necessary for teaching to earn full professional status.

The road ahead will not be easy. No other profession has faced quite the same dilemma in its quest for professionalization. Doctors and lawyers practice their profession, for the most part, unobserved by both clients and the public. There is a mystery surrounding what they do, and few would assert it could be done by persons untrained in those professional cultures. Teachers, on the other hand, are fully visible to students each and every day and, for the most part, the public perceives, even if incorrectly, that it knows what teachers do almost as well as teachers themselves.

In a speech delivered to the Jubilee Convocation of the College of Education of the University of Saskatchewan, Robert Howsam, one of the leading advocates of professional status for teaching, stated:

> For the most part professionals play but small parts in the lives of their clients. They are called in to help in some crisis such as illness or legal entanglement, provide the service, and depart. Or they come to solve a problem such as designing a house or building a bridge. It is not intended that they impact directly the lives of those whom they serve.
> In the teaching profession the situation is different. Our service is developmental rather than crisis resolving or clinical. To be effective we have to be involved in intervention on a continuous and prolonged basis during the span of life when children and youth are most impressionable and vulnerable. We fashion peoples' lives and influence their futures. We tinker with their values, their beliefs, and their behaviors. Small wonder that people are sensitive to our power and concerned over our competence.[1]

Howsam goes on to suggest that the public may have difficulty tolerating a profession which views the preparation of children and youth to live in a changing society as one of its major responsibilities.

> It is becoming increasingly clear to me that the teaching profession is caught in a continuing struggle ... between traditional and emergent values, between relative closedness and openness to reality and new experience....
> As we strive for actualization as a unique profession, we can be certain that whatever we are we will have to develop and display a professional culture; be vigorous advocates of knowledge and the inherent human right to possess it; be spokesman for the right of children and youth to be prepared for their world regardless of desires to keep them in our own or those of our ancestors; press for schools that favor openness and respect the dignity and worth of children; and both espouse and demonstrate in our own behavior a lifelong quest for learning.[2]

It is not difficult to interpret Howsam's comments as a message with special meaning for social studies teachers. Nowhere in the curriculum are the issues he raises more likely to be confronted than in the social studies classroom. Of the teachers who will bear the responsibility for and the repercussions of moving teaching toward professional status, few will bear a fuller measure than social studies teachers.

The advocates of competency based teacher education view it as a viable means through which to professionalize teaching. They do not, however, claim that CBTE can address all of the challenges confronting the development of teaching as a profession. It cannot, for example, be expected to become a major force in the quest for increased autonomy for the profession. Yet CBTE's emphases on explicit definition of teaching competence and on the criterion referenced assessment of competency demonstration are major steps in the right direction. Through these concepts CBTE can be expected to further the development of at least two of the major characteristics associated with professional status—the development of a body of knowledge and repertoire of behaviors clearly identified and associated with the effective practice of teaching and the development of agreed upon performance standards for admission to and continuance within the profession. Many who support and continue efforts to develop the CBTE movement do so in the belief that its greatest contribution will be toward this purpose.

Readers should not expect to find CBTE treated extensively

as a strategy for teacher preparation in this volume. While Part Two will introduce the uninitiated to the basic concepts of CBTE, this volume primarily examines CBTE with a twofold purpose: to illuminate the movement from the perspective of the development of teaching as a profession and to highlight those challenges especially relevant to social studies teaching.

Footnotes
[1] Robert B. Howsam, "The Trails That Ships Make in the Water," (Speech presented to the Jubilee Convocation of the College of Education, University of Saskatchewan, October 15, 1977), p. 7.
[2] *Ibid.*, p. 8.

Part One

Professionalizing Social Studies Teaching

The teaching profession is plagued by a lack of self-confidence. Social studies teachers are doubly plagued. Not only is there little empirical evidence to guide "how they teach," there is also confusion about "what they should teach." The profession is also plagued by a lack of public trust. The public's increasing disenchantment with education, the continued clamor for "accountability," angry allegations that the achievement of students is declining in just about every subject are no secrets. Too often, the result is a buffeting of teaching and teachers by social pressures which wax and wane with each passing crisis.

This will undoubtedly continue until what teachers do can be clearly established as making a difference in what happens to learners. It will continue as long as the public lacks confidence that teachers possess the competence to assume primary responsibility for deciding what shall be taught; what children and youth should learn.

It is not likely that the problems associated with professionalizing social studies teaching will be solved in the near future. As Robert Howsam points out in Chapter 1, deeply entrenched societal forces stand as obstacles to the full acceptance of teaching as a profession. The basic controversy is "whether traditional or emergent values are to govern the right to learn and the right to teach."

What are the purposes of social studies? The public expects social studies to "socialize" children for effective participation in society. Yet the beliefs, attitudes, and customs valued by society are often confused and confusing. This confusion means that social studies teachers must either assume major responsibility for deciding what shall be taught or accept a curriculum reduced to the lowest common denominator.

The bases for making such decisions are not clear, however. Social studies educators do not agree as to what the purposes of social studies should be. Yet it is crucial that these purposes be clear if the professionalization of social studies teaching is ever to occur. In Chapter 2, John Jarolimek addresses this issue through an examination of what is *basic* in social studies. Through analysis of what should happen to children as a result of social studies teaching, he develops a thoughtful and convincing statement of the purpose of social studies.

How does any of this relate to competency based teacher education? The transmission of a professional culture for teaching depends upon the quality of programs designed to prepare teachers. Given time, a body of validated knowledge to guide the practice of teaching will be developed. Given time, consensus will be reached concerning the purposes of social studies. Teacher education must be held accountable for the preparation of *competent* professionals.

CBTE is characterized by explicitly stated goals and objectives, by publicly known criteria and procedures for the assessment of achievement, by the capacity to collect data on the effects of instruction and to use these data as the basis for the revision and regeneration of programs to prepare teachers. In other words, CBTE is confronting many of the most crucial issues in professionalizing teaching.

1 Challenges in Professionalizing Social Studies Teaching

Robert B. Howsam

Introduction

It is the aspiration and intent of this volume to apply the principles and practices of competency based education (CBE) and competency based teacher education (CBTE) to the preparation of social studies teachers. In the endeavor the presently foremost process of the social studies—*Inquiry*—will be used. The challenge can only be viewed as great since CBE seeks precision in goals and objectives while social studies to date has defied even a simple consensual definition.[1]

Even if social studies scholars and educators were able to agree on a definition and a delimitation of their field, the problem of consensus would not be resolved. Nothing in the school curriculum (except perhaps sex education and the nature of creation) is so generative of controversy between the educator and segments of the public as is the substance of the social studies and the right to teach it.[2]

Competency based education is distinguished by its concern for goals and objectives, for making them explicit and public, for providing instructional opportunities which enable attainment of the objectives, for learner accountability, and for regenerative processes based upon data and feedback. It is systemic. It recognizes the intricacies of instructional systems and strives to design a complex of learning-teaching elements which are compatible one with the other and with the whole and its purposes.

Neither systems nor CBE live comfortably with ambiguities and uncertainties. Social studies is marked by controversy which extends all the way from societal differences over the purpose and function of the school to the content and method of the studies. It can be stated with some confidence that the social studies will not and cannot come fully into its own unless and until there is reasonable resolution of these ambiguities and conflicts. Neither will it be found easy to adapt CBE to them or them to CBE.

Stating the difficulties, however, does not in any way alleviate the need. The society, the schools, and our children and youth need the social studies more today than ever before in our history. This need can only be predicted to increase. The issues to be faced are not to be found primarily within the social studies. Rather they are societal and in large measure have their origin within the controversy over whether traditional or emergent values are to govern the right to learn and the right to teach. Though the social studies teaching and social studies curricula tend to be the focus of attention, the issues should not be permitted to rest therein. Rather, they should be the concern of all in the teaching profession and of all who perceive the school as an important agent in the processes of social adaptation as well as in the processes of enculturation. The function of the school in American society, the very existence of teaching as a profession, and important commitments of the society to openness and freedom are at stake.

The Growing Need and Prospect

Despite the problems still to be confronted, there is a growing prospect—however yet dimly perceived—that the social studies will emerge in the 1980s as the most important single contribution to the school experience after the need for the development of literacy has been met. This will be in response to perceived needs. American education always has been responsive to the major stresses and thrusts of the times.

In the late 1950s and the 1960s, science and mathematics were front and center on the educational stage. Upstaged by Sputnik and frightened by the prospect of Soviet superiority in science and technology, the nation threw its resources into upgrading and retooling the science teaching and curricula. The National Science Foundation was established; and it set about upgrading the science teachers in their content areas, developing and disseminating new science curricula, and encouraging more young people to elect science options at school and select science as a career. By the late 1960s the NSF efforts in this direction had run their course. Belatedly it was recognized that knowledge of science is but one side of the professional teacher coin. The other—the science and art of teaching—had been neglected.

Attention then turned to developing the professional aspects of teaching. Though generally marked by modest appropriations, a number of program efforts were mounted. The Elementary Models Project, Triple-T, EPDA and Teacher Corps are examples of teacher education thrust. These too subsided and dwindled until in the second half of the decade of the seventies little is left. Sharing the emphasis during this period were other crisis-motivated efforts such as occupational education, multicultural education, and bilingual education.

As history is written, the seventies are likely to be viewed as years during which long-term future trends emerged. The decade produced the energy and pollution crises which portend changes in lifestyles of great societal significance. It produced Watergate and other evidence of economic and political behavior inimical to the interests of a healthy society. Much seeming progress was made in resolving some of the great social problems of our times, but evidence of societal malfunctions and nonfunctions grew in scope as well as scale. Perhaps most important of all, evidence began to emerge that the world finally might be beginning to take seriously the global-system nature of problems and the need for global solutions.[3]

Regardless of the specifics of change, it can be anticipated that the society will once again call upon the schools to play a major role in the re-education process. Learning to live in new ways calls for social education. The social studies has this as its area of responsibility. The 1980s could be the years of N.S.S.F. even as the sixties were of N.S.F.

It will be difficult to meet the challenges to the social studies unless its professionals and its scholars together can confront a series of problems and issues, arrive at agreement on solution, and succeed in negotiating with the American People for a new role and function for the social studies and the social studies teacher. Given success in the social studies endeavor, the need to refashion the curriculum and redevelop social studies teachers will emerge.

The Contribution of CBE

There is in competency based education and its application to teacher preparation (CBTE) no magic solution to the problems of confusion and conflict over role and function as they exist within the social studies as a teaching field. Competency approaches assume the existence of at least reasonable agreement on societal goals. Given such agreement it is possible to generate specific objectives which derive from the goals and are consistent with them. Once that has been achieved, it is possible to develop delivery and assessment processes which, regeneratively used, can successively approximate criterion levels of achievement and cause the society to be appreciative of the school as an institution and the contribution which the social studies makes.

Competency based approaches do, however, have tremendous capacity to force identification and confrontation of issues. No previous approach to instructional development has had an equal capacity to examine all elements of the system and to design and redesign until a workable system is achieved or the elements which inhibit achievement have been identified.

Statements of limitation such as the above have reference to the global, large-order problems which frustrate the social studies educators. They have no relevance when the problem is to do effectively whatever it is that has been the object of agreement. The large problems stand in the way of full realization for the social studies. Day-to-day and year-to-year satisfactions have more to do with making the best of what we have. Competency based education whether applied to school or to teacher education has a powerful capacity to help us make the best of what we have.

The School as an Institution

Education and enculturation are functions that are basic to every society. Arrangements to meet such needs are universal among cultures and range from largely informal structure and role definition in simple societies to complex systems of institutions and roles in some modern societies. The school as an institution is a societal invention designed to assist the society in the enculturation, education, and occupational preparation of children and youth.

Societies differ in their locus of the authority to educate. Some operate highly centralized systems with curricula, teacher education, examinations, standards, and other functions controlled centrally by the nation or by states. In such a case the larger society takes unto itself the right to determine what education a child shall have. In others, such as our own, considerable responsibility is devolved upon the home and the local community, even though higher levels of government may share in or delimit the processes. Accidents of history may be as significant as conscious design in the origin of the selected emphasis. Once in place, however, there is strong resistance to shifts towards either greater or lesser degrees of local control. Our society has made its choice; the schools by design and desire are kept close to the people.

Societies are characterized by two types of institutions—*primary* and *secondary*. Primary institutions are found in all societies; they are the most fundamental form of social organization and comprise the home, the church, the school, and the overall village or community. Their functions are to ensure the survival of the community and of its ways. The tribal village represents the community in its simplest and perhaps most pure form. It and its institutionalized or role-delegated functions preserve and protect. It is culture preservative and change resistant. The village walls, whether physically or only socially present, identify those who belong as insiders in contradistinction to those who do not belong and are strangers. "Truth" as perceived within is taught within;[4] heresy is kept out. Norms of behavior are specified and enforced.

Regardless of what happens to a society as it grows and develops, the effort continues to raise its children to conform to the norms of their elders. Schools and churches are expected to reinforce home and community values and behaviors. Failure to support may be tolerated, but subversion of community values, beliefs, and behaviors will not.

As societies grow in size and complexity, specialization of roles and function occurs; this moves some of the functions outside of the capacity of primary institutions and communities. This brings about the establishment of *secondary institutions*. One definition of a secondary institution is that it is not *primary*. It tends to be change, rather than culture preservative, in orientation. Though it may be educative in its endeavors, it does not have that as a societal function. It is not responsive to local control. Transportation and the automotive industry can be used to represent the array of secondary institutions that have grown up in America in response to multiple needs and opportunities. They, along with communication, recreation, and other industries, transformed the way of life and brought down the village walls in the process. Where the child was once the child of a village, he now is the child of Marshall McLuhan's *global village*. He is, in all but the most remote and isolated areas of our society and the world, subject to secondary institution exposure to the ideas, lifestyles, values, and behaviors of the entire world. He travels around the globe, and his planetary fellow citizens are almost equally mobile. By satellite the world events of the day come to his home as a dinnertime event. Whereas the village child lived in a relatively closed and restrictive environment (whether by design or just by force of circumstance), the global village child confronts an openness not previously known in any society.

Among the serious problems facing the social studies are the resolution of the issue of whether the child is to be viewed as belonging to the primary institution village or to the global village and whether the teacher represents the village or the broader society. Closely involved in this issue are the rights of the child to learn and to be prepared to cope with the global village which will impact him.

Can the social studies teacher be less than well informed, experienced, well educated, and skilled in the processes of effective teaching? Can the social studies professionals be less than advocates of the right to learn and the right to be effective world citizens? On the other hand, are social studies educators confident of their capacity to preserve for children and youth those elements of primary institution life which have long been mainstays of societal process and individual well-being, while at the same time keeping open for all the right to become as well as to be.

It is not for social studies educators alone to answer these questions. It would appear, however, that the very nature of their studies places upon them a disproportionate share of responsibility for pressing the issues. Mathematics teachers have the issue of metrics against traditional measurements, but in the long run the issue is relatively inconsequential when contrasted with issues of national or international society or experimental lifestyles as contrasted with traditional. The sciences may teach of nuclear energy, but the issues of morality and human consequence are more likely to be raised in social studies discussions. In the last analysis the abrasive areas of interface between local culture and the school are the social studies first, followed well back perhaps by literature and health education.

What competencies, then, will social studies teachers need? Clearly this is not known in the absence of a more definitive and less equivocating societal role for the school. Despite this, however, it is still possible to set objectives for professional social studies teachers. Knowledge objectives (cognitive), behaviors and skills to be mastered, and affective domain values, attitudes, and beliefs are not much if any different for teaching in a primary or a secondary institution setting. The teacher needs to have them in order to make professional decisions as to their use. The real difference is in the skills of sensing the local culture and staying sufficiently within its bounds to survive and to be as effective as conditions permit. Additional skills—not usually recognized or consciously developed—are in the area of negotiating with the local community and of affecting local limits through influence.

Teaching as a Profession

A seeming anomaly is the existence of a profession serving within a primary institution. Professions are secondary institutions. They are established for the purpose of expanding the capacity of their members to serve society in their respective areas of expertise, and they are made relatively independent of direct control by the client or the public in order that professional decisions may be as valid, as free from conventional wisdom and lay control, as possible.[5]

In the early American community the teacher was an extension of the home and community. No preparation was required. The community exercised direct surveillance through a Visitors Committee and indirect control through the individual families. A major criterion of employment was fitting in with local values and ways. Subsequent developments have added some professional preparation and raised the general level of education for teachers, but selection and preparation still favor the "safe" teacher with local community compatability.

Professionals have two sources of authority.[6] One derives from the client or employer, the other from the profession. The client or employer grants to the practitioner professional the right to practice or serve in the specific case or situation. The responsibility for practicing professionally is on the other hand derived from the organized profession, and accountability for ethics and competence is to and through the profession. This duality in accountability has worked reasonably well in the other professions (despite modern problems in the system of delivery of and payment for such services). It has not worked well in teaching, however. Whether it can be made to work to the mutual advantage of both the teacher and the client remains to be seen.

One of the reasons for the dual source of authority not seeming to fit the teaching profession lies in the concept of the school as a primary institution. Under the primary institution assumption the client is the immediate community and the family. Their interests are paramount and they control the school as an institution.[7] To date, teachers, other than those in higher education institutions, have had little success in the pursuit of academic and/or professional freedom. In considerable part this may be due to restrictions imposed because of the maturity level of the students and to the fact of compulsory exposure (attendance). The public may sense or believe that the immature should not be required to submit to mind-enlarging and values-questioning processes at the hands of a professional teacher.

A further difference in situation may account for public reluctance to make teachers professionally, rather than publicly, accountable. This is the fact that the established professions characteristically are engaged in *preserving* the well-being of the client in times of crisis (illness, criminal charges, litigation), while the teacher and the school are given long-term *developmental* responsibilities. In the case of the teacher the responsibility is different, more intensive and extensive, and presumably greater. Certainly it involves a different kind of relationship.

Despite public reluctance to accept new roles for teachers, the issue of professional status for teachers already has been joined. Teachers through their organizations are pressing strongly for professional recognition and for the rights, privileges, and responsibilities which professional status confers. Professional governance bills are being promoted in many states. Collective negotiation rights already have been won in almost one half of the states. Increasingly these rights include negotiating over conditions of work, including curriculum development and the right to teach free from administrative or other interference.

On the other side, citizen groups are springing up all across the nation and pressing through activist strategies for "a return of the schools to the people." Some of this development has been deliberately fostered in the disadvantaged communities, but indications are that the strategy will be most effective in the typical suburban setting where its use is growing rapidly. The Institute for Responsive Education is an example of efforts to arouse the citizenry. Its publication reports successes in various communities and exhorts others to take up the cause. A recent issue carried a contributed item with a statement which is characteristic of the issues as perceived by people of that mind:

> Further evidence of citizen frustration over lack of accessibility and responsiveness on the part of school officials was uncovered by the NCCS Commission on School Governance.
> In 1974–75 the Commission heard testimony in five major cities on

who controls the public schools. Among the conclusions: lay control continues to erode; professionals wield an overbalance of power in the schools.[8]

It appears probable that efforts such as these will be common for the foreseeable future. What the long-term impact will be can only be speculated.

The greatest single deterrent to acceptance of the teaching profession into the societal company of the other professions is not to be found in community conflict, however. Rather it is to be found in the dismal state of the professional culture of teachers. "Professional Culture" is a term used by the AACTE Bicentennial Commission[9] to designate the body of knowledge and the repertoire of behaviors and skills which the profession has built up through its history, transmits to the inductees during the preparation process, and uses in the practice of the profession. Without such a culture the profession lacks the basis for both public and self-trust and confidence, and so cannot expect to be granted professional status. Teachers themselves have attested to their reliance on personal experience in the absence of a valid body of professional knowledge.[10] They reported that they had learned little in teacher education and shared professional problems to a minimum extent with other teachers. Supervisors and principals were found to be of little help. The teachers had worked out their own strategies, had survived, and continued to "make out" independently and in relative isolation.

Both resulting from and contributing to the lack of professional culture for the teaching profession are the neglect of teacher effectiveness and other educational research and the lack of adequate "Life Space" within which to prepare teachers. This situation prevails at pre-service, in-service, and continuing education levels. Both time and support resources are seriously suboptimal.

All of us in the teaching profession have inherited the consequences of decades of unconscionable neglect of teaching as a professional study and the school as an object of conscious and purposive design. Once again, the problem in part at least originates in the notion of the school as a primary institution to be kept close to the community at all costs. Such an approach works well enough under the conditions of simpler times but it threatens the very survival of the school in times of the global village.

All teachers, including those of the social studies, are affected by the prevailing situation in the teaching profession.

Teachers cannot hope to be effective in the absence of well developed generic skills of teaching and specialized expertise in the instructional strategies of their particular teaching field. Neither can they expect to be competent without an extensive, thorough, and relevant professional education, both pre-service and continuing. Without demonstrated capacity they are unlikely as a group to convince the public that they should be permitted to exercise their judgments about the learning experiences students should have. This is particularly true of social studies teachers, since they deal directly in areas of social issues and public disagreements.

The AACTE Bicentennial Commission recommended that the profession should concentrate its energies on developing a genuine professional culture and making it a part of the behavioral repertoire of teachers. It advocated the immediate addition of one year to the preparation period and the adoption of the year of internship as a universal requirement before professional certification. If the competencies needed by professional teachers are to be required of all who enter the profession, nothing less will be even minimally adequate. It will not be easy for either teachers or the public to refashion the image and expectation of the teaching profession, but it must be done. An institution is never better than the people who serve within it. A suboptimal profession is a formula for a troubled and inadequate school.

Teacher Education for the Social Studies

Social studies, for teacher education purposes, is a teaching field which is comprised of selected materials and methodologies from a number of related *disciplines*. Alternatively it may be viewed as an examination of human experience and behavior, past and present, from the selected perspectives of disciplines in the humanities and social and behavioral sciences with the purpose of attainment of identified learning objectives in the area of social behavior and citizenship.

Teaching, for our purposes, is a professional act wherein through the use of educated expertise desired behavior in learners is optimally achieved.

It has been stated that social studies is a set of goals.[11] This is, of course, a statement which adds nothing to understanding. More useful would be a statement that the social studies curriculum is a set of goals together with the means for achieving them. But this too has little utility, since it places no boundary around that which is social or social studies as contrasted, for example, with mathematics or natural science.

Nonetheless, the use of goals as the basis for a definition does have utility in that it indicates the presence of value and of purpose. This is the approach of competency based education. It starts with a selection of goals from amongst the available alternatives. Having done so, it is possible to proceed to translate the goals into objectives and develop the assessment and delivery systems needed for goal attainment.

The approach needed in developing a preparation program for social studies teachers is precisely the same. The goals and objectives can be expected to fall into several groups based upon the types of expertise which will be needed:

1. Mastery to a "safe" level of the generic knowledge, behaviors, skills, attitudes, and values which at any given point in time are expected of those who are accepted as members of the teaching profession and certified as teachers (generic competencies).
2. Particular strength in those professional competencies needed in teaching the social studies (specialized competencies).
3. Knowledge and skills from the content disciplines upon which the social studies draws to a level adequate for effectiveness (teaching field[s]).
4. Knowledge of the disciplines upon which the teaching profession depends for its scientific and scholarly insights (undergirding disciplines).
5. Awareness and understanding of current social, political, and economic problems of the society and of the contribution which the disciplines make to the understanding of the problems, combined with the ability to relate the two (events literacy).
6. Multicultural and pluralistic awareness and respect, particularly with regard to groups represented in the community of service, to the end that individual students from differing backgrounds will be understood, valued, and professionally taught.
7. Ability to sense the values and identities of interest groups in the community and to act in such a way as to retain both the confidence of the community and the right and freedom to teach professionally.
8. Awareness of and commitment to the teaching profession.
9. A capacity to continue to grow and develop through experience and continued formal and informal education throughout the professional career.

The mere listing of these challenges is indicative of the need for expanded life space for teacher education. Those of us who attempt to develop objectives from the list and instruction to produce the competencies quickly discover the inadequacy of present conditions. Nonetheless, the need for an instructional system which is capable of delivering on these competencies exists whether the opportunity is present or not. Confronting the challenge may be the best way to produce action.

Urgency

Teaching the social studies may be perceived as the highest privilege which society grants to any of its many kinds of professionals. The learner comes to the social studies both to be enculturated and to be freed from enculturation. The ultimate objective is the person who is responsibly free, a valuing and rational being with a sense of his past and a quest for a meaningful and rewarding future. The social studies teacher presides over processes out of which lives are shaped and societies influenced.

The United States of America was born out of conflict and revolution. Its historic documents bespeak determination to be free and equal. Implicit and explicit in the American way of life is the need and right to be informed and to make choices and decisions based upon knowledge and values, subject only to consideration for others and for the common good. It is to the processes by which such decisions are made and to the background for making them that social studies is addressed. The decisions themselves rest with the individual who has the right to decide whether the culture from which he came was right or wrong, to be preserved and followed or changed.

The power to influence through the social studies is tremendous. Small wonder, then, that the society has kept and continues to keep a watchful eye on what goes on within it. The trouble with watchfulness is that it often is distorted into behavior on the part of intense individuals or groups which, passionately and/or politically expressed, supplants the general public will. The consequence frequently is a process of reductionism which leaves in the curriculum only those materials and strategies about which there is not disagreement. The result tends to be instruction which is bland and inconsequential; evidence of this condition in the school curriculum is readily available to those who wish to see. The secondary institutions—relatively free of direct monitoring and control—inform, stimulate, and challenge people with information and ideas from all over the world. They also use the most effective available modes of communication.

Because of this and because of other breakdowns and developments in our society, more than ever before our children and youth need the opportunity to examine openly societal issues in the presence of wise, informed, and skilled adults. The greatest and most universally available opportunity for this is at school, and the best prepared people for the role should be the teacher and particularly the social studies teacher. That the society does not grant the complete role for teachers and even demand it is one of the tragedies of our educational system and our society.

The situation will not change rapidly, but every effort should be made to nudge it in the desired direction. Interactively, attention to the following could bring about substantially early progress:

1. Intensive governmental, university, and professional efforts to enlarge and improve the knowledge and skills base for the teaching profession (professional culture). The level of public trust in any profession is directly related to its level of competence.
2. Upgrading the preparation of entering teachers through preservice.
3. Determined action among social studies educators to arrive at a workable consensus on what the social studies is and what its goals and objectives are.
4. Strong and continuous effort to involve the public to enlighten it as to the situation which exists within the profession, and to enlist support for a revised role for the school and for the social studies.
5. Massive upgrading of the teaching profession in the direction of full professionalization with the privileges and responsibilities common to the professions.
6. Vigorous assertion on the part of teachers of the right of people to know and to learn and of the critical need for freedom to teach responsibly in the public schools.

Failure to make dramatic progress within a relatively short period of time will threaten the continued existence of our system of public education which is based upon prepared and certified teachers. Public confidence already is seriously eroded, and the evidence of disaffection has grown. Yet the profession continues in its failure to state the problems and declare the issues. It is time to open the entire system to scrutiny, and to do so in the faith that the people want effective education too. Since the problems of education and of the teaching profession reach their most dramatic level in the social studies, what better platform could there be?

Footnotes

[1] James L. Barth and S. Samuel Shermis, "Defining the Social Studies: An Exploration of Three Traditions," *Social Education* (November, 1970), pp. 743–751.

[2] Bruce Joyce has listed six areas of our culture that are particularly tabooed from examination in schools. See Bruce R. Joyce, *New Strategies for Social Education* (Chicago: Science Research Associates, 1972), pp. 5–6.

[3] See for example: 1. Reshaping International Order (RIO Report), *A Report to the Club of Rome* (New York: E. P. Dutton, 1976) and 2. John M. and Magna Cordell McHale with introduction by Harlan Cleveland, *Basic Human Needs: A Framework for Action*. Report to the United Nations Environmental Program by the Center for the Integrative Studies (University of Houston, April 1977).

[4] For a lighter and pleasurable allusion to this, listen again to *Fiddler on the Roof* and *South Pacific*.

[5] See Robert B. Howsam, Dean C. Corrigan, George W. Denmark, and Robert J. Nash, *Educating a Profession*. Bicentennial Commission report to the American Association of Colleges for Teacher Education (Washington, D.C.: The Association, 1976), p. 176. Chapter One includes a twelve-point list of characteristics of a profession.

[6] Myron Lieberman, *Education as a Profession* (Englewood Cliffs, New Jersey: Prentice-Hall, 1956).

[7] The assumption that the student is client and that the right to learn derives from a larger societal unit would make a major difference in the role of professional teacher. Similarly, an assumption that a larger societal unit such as a nation or a world body had the dominant interest and the right to override local or individual preferences would and does make a major difference.

This issue has been made real at the international level by President Carter's speaking against the treatment of individuals and minorities in other countries. Would not a logical extension of this idea eventually lead to examination of what children experience in school?

[8] Chrissie Bamber, "Call toll free 800 NET-WORK when your child's school system is more system than school," *Citizen Action in Education* (May 1977), p. 5.

[9] Howsam et al., *Educating a Profession*.

[10] Don C. Lortie, *Schoolteacher* (Chicago, Illinois: University of Chicago Press, 1975).

[11] James L. Barth and S. Samuel Shermis, *ibid.*, p. 744.

2 The Basics in Social Studies: Implications for the Preparation of Teachers

John Jarolimek

Introduction

The subject of what is basic in social studies education is so complex and controversial and so susceptible to varied interpretations that it is impossible to discuss it in a way that will satisfy all readers. Indeed, for reasons that will soon become apparent, it is not likely that *any* thoughtful reader will agree with all that is said here. Perhaps this essay will have served its purpose if it will provoke readers to think through, defend, and articulate their own views on what is basic in social studies education.

We use the adjective *basic* here in the sense of somethings being fundamental or essential. This being the case, components of the school curriculum considered to be *basic* are required to be taught to and learned by all, assuming, of course, that learners are sufficiently competent intellectually to do so. This suggests that basic learnings are *common* to all who attend school. It implies that the learners would be required to demonstrate an acceptable level of competent performance before being certified as having completed the basic learning. It is logically inconsistent for basic learnings to be offered as electives.

When the term *the basics* is used, reference is usually made to fundamental literacy skills—reading, writing, and arithmetical operations. These learnings are judged to be *basic* in the sense that without them the individual would be handicapped in his or her ability to learn other things. Without having command of these basic skills, the individual would also be handicapped as an adult in conducting the activities of ordinary living in a society that relies so heavily on written communication and quantitative operations in conducting its business. Clearly, these *basics* are of direct benefit to individuals and are indirectly beneficial to society. Few would dispute their importance or the school's responsibility to help young people develop them. With the exception of those children with severe physical, mental, or neurological disorders that would prevent them from doing so, *all* children and youth could be expected to learn these basics at an acceptable, minimum level. It has been suggested that this "floor" (the achievement level below which no child would be allowed to fall) should be "the threshold to the realm of work."[1]

There is no question that the social studies can and often does contribute to the development of these basic skills.[2] Much of social studies beyond the primary grades is learned through reading. This contact with printed material in social studies can be used to enhance the learner's reading ability. Likewise, oral and written reports, outlining, researching topics, and dealing with quantitative relationships in social studies can be used to develop basic skills. Most specialists in social studies *and* in the skills fields encourage this type of integrated teaching. It should be recognized, however, that such a teaching practice, although beneficial, has nothing to do with what is basic in the social studies field.

Professional educators and lay persons alike often perceive what is basic in social studies as being related in some direct way to citizenship education. This relationship is rooted in a functionalist or social order theory of education, which holds that education socializes young people into the existing social order.[3] The idea, doubtless of ancient origin, was articulated by John Dewey near the turn of the century and has been widely accepted by American curriculum planners and social theorists:

> If a plague carried off the members of a society all at once, it is obvious that the group would be permanently done for. Yet the death of each of its constituent members is as certain as if an epidemic took them all at once. But the graded difference in age, the fact that some are born as some die, makes possible through transmission of ideas and practices the constant reweaving of the social fabric. Yet this renewal is not automatic. Unless pains are taken to see that genuine and thorough transmission takes place, the most civilized group will relapse into barbarism and then into savagery. In fact, the human young are so immature that if they were left to themselves without the guidance and succor of others, they could not acquire the rudimentary abilities necessary for physical existence. The young of human beings compare so poorly in original efficiency with the young of many of the lower animals, that even the powers needed for physical sustenation have to be acquired

under tuition. How much more, then, is this the case with respect to all the technological, artistic, scientific, and moral achievements of humanity![4]

In more recent years, Jerome S. Bruner makes somewhat the same point:

> ... Culture, thus, is not discovered; it is passed on or forgotten. All this suggests to me that we had better be cautious in talking about the method of discovery, or discovery as the principal vehicle of education. Simply from a biological point of view, it does not seem to be the case at all. We ought to be extremely careful, therefore, to think about the range of possible techniques used for guaranteeing that we produce competent adults within a society that the educational process supports. Thus, in order to train these adults, education must program their development of skills, and provide them with models, if you will, of the environment. All of these things must be taken into account, rather than just taking it for granted that discovery is a principal way in which the individual finds out about his environment.[5]

These authors, and others like them, are saying that there are some essential elements of the culture that need to be passed on from one generation to the next if the society is to survive. The questions this raises, among others, are "What elements?" and "Are any of them in the province of social studies education?"

To answer these questions and to answer the more fundamental question, "What is basic?", one needs criteria in order to make an objective judgment as to what qualifies as basic and what does not. That is, how else can one tell if something is "basic"? If one does not have objective criteria, one person's opinion is about as good as the next person's. If there is no way of assessing what deserves higher priority than something else, then everything must be given equal weight. This is obviously not a desirable plan of action, for under such an arrangement a trivial event in history would be equated with a major trend. Educators have been struggling with the problem of identifying criteria for selecting content of the curriculum long before 1859 when Herbert Spencer published his often-cited essay entitled "What Knowledge Is of Most Worth?" They have enjoyed only moderate success in this effort.

Our problem in defining what is basic—or even establishing criteria for such definitions—is that there is no consensus concerning the major, overall goals of education. Not only is there lack of consensus, but different constituents embrace goals that are incompatible with those of other constituents. Thus, if one group is accommodated by what is taught as basic, others are at the same time alienated. As an example of contradictory goals, here are a few of the stated purposes of American education that appear in the literature:

1. Fundamentally, education is for the intellectual development of the individual; it is not for the purpose of the State.
2. Schools exist not to prepare individuals, but to direct the course of social change.
3. The schools should prepare individuals to serve the needs of society; i.e., schooling is directed toward the development of effective citizenship.
4. The school's main purpose is to meet the interests and needs of learners.
5. Schools are vehicles for the development of human resources; they should stress job training and certification functions.
6. The role of the school is to sort and allocate human resources in accordance with manpower needs of the nation and to train youth to become part of a compliant labor force.

With such disparity of views on the basic purpose and thrust of public education, it is impossible to identify what is basic in a way that will get general support. We shall attempt to work our way through this thicket by stating certain axioms that have to do with society and social life and then extract criteria from those axioms. This is followed by samples of subject matter and/or experiences that might be used to achieve the basic learnings.

Defining What Is Basic in Social Studies

This section presents six axioms relating to human societies as social systems. Whereas the axioms may be regarded as self-evident propositions, each is discussed in accordance with the purposes of this chapter. The axioms and the accompanying discussion of them provide the basis for the identification of criteria to be used in determining what is basic to social studies education in elementary and secondary schools. Each criterion statement is followed by a list of possible subject matter and learning experiences. These elements of subject matter and learning experiences are suggested only as *illustrative* of the type of content and activities that could be used in achieving basic learnings in social studies education.

Axiom 1. *The infant human being has the innate capacity to develop in immensely diverse ways.*

One cannot study human beings and their cultures without being fascinated by their diversity. Because of their unique ability to make cultural adaptations to their surroundings, human beings inhabit every conceivable place on earth. Even the most hostile environments—bitter cold or scorching hot—do not escape human habitation. In the area of communication, linguists estimate that the world's people speak more than 3000 languages plus that many or more dialects. Over and over again we are reminded that the range of human potentialities seems almost to be infinite.

What is so meaningful about this adaptive quality is that any individual human being has at the moment of birth the innate capacity to live in any one of the world's cultures, to learn any one or more of its 3000 languages, to be identified with any national group, or to embrace any of an indefinitely large number of religious beliefs. The fact that a person learns to live as people do in France, Zambia, Mexico, China, the United States, or anywhere else can be accounted for by the fact that the person was born and "brought up" (i.e. socialized) in that particular culture. Except for an accident of birth, the individual might have been born somewhere else and become a member of some other culture.

Societies go to great lengths to ensure that their young people grow up behaving and acting the way others in their society do, and not the way a foreigner would. If a sizable number of English children grew up behaving and acting as Russian children, one would have to conclude that there was something seriously wrong with the system of socializing children in the English society. If the socializing mechanisms are functioning properly, they will produce a certain degree of similarity in the behavior patterns of all individuals. This is what makes communication, interaction, and, indeed, group life itself possible. This is also what gives a society its distinctiveness. This is how it is possible to distinguish between people of Iceland and people of Afghanistan, for instance. The similarities in what people in a society know and value are referred to as their *common culture*. It is obvious that a major responsibility of an educational system of a society is to prepare individuals to participate in the common mainstream culture.

There are many things that children learn in school that go beyond elements of the mainstream culture. For example, a youngster may learn a second language in a bilingual program. This is commendable and is a richly rewarding learning. But it is not essential in our culture that a child knows a second language. It may be convenient but it is not crucial. It *is* essential that he or she knows English, however, because the language of the mainstream culture is English. Not to be fluent in English would severely restrict the life choices an individual could make. Such a person would have opportunities for advanced education foreclosed, job opportunities greatly reduced, and the ability to interact with others extremely limited.

Much of what we call the mainstream culture directly involves the substance of social studies education. The economic system, to which one's livelihood is attached, is an example. Another is the law and justice systems that touch the life of every citizen from before birth to after death. The fundamental rights that citizens enjoy—life itself, liberty, and the pursuit of happiness, and others—are deeply imbedded in the mainstream culture. To the extent that citizens are ignorant of such elements of the culture, they are crippled in their ability to participate in a social legacy that is rightfully theirs. Of course, some of these learnings can be achieved through ordinary living outside of school. But no modern society anywhere in the world is willing to take the risk of using incidental life experiences as a primary vehicle for socializing persons into the mainstream culture. In this country, at this point in time, the elementary and secondary schools can and must accept much of the responsibility for teaching young people how to participate in the common culture. The social studies program is crucial in achieving that goal.

What is basic?

Criterion 1:
   In the social studies those values, skills, processes, experiences, or subject matter can be considered *basic* if they teach the learners to participate in the common culture.

Possible subject matter and/or learning experiences
Subject matter:
   1. Sources of the American heritage.
   2. The economic system.
   3. The law and justice systems.
   4. The political system.
   5. Culture-bearing institutions.
   6. Cross-cultural, comparative studies.

7. The development of American ideals and institutions; local, state, and national history.
8. Individual economic responsibilities; career education; the world of work.

Learning experiences:
1. Using study skills and work habits such as locating and gathering information from a variety of sources; reading social studies materials for various purposes; using maps, globes, charts, graphs; organizing information into usable structures, such as outlining, taking notes, keeping records; conducting an inquiry on a problem of interest.
2. Analyzing information presented through the news media: distinguishing between fact and opinion; recognizing bias in advertising, political statements, "news" stories.
3. Participating in real-life experiences dealing with the political, law and justice, and economic systems.

Axiom 2. *The shared values of a society provide the basis for common group goal setting and thereby are essential in promoting cohesiveness and identification with the group.*

In order for a society to survive, it must have a set of core values for which there is general support. Without such consensus on basic values, the society would be torn with dissension and would find itself in turmoil much of the time. Individuals must be able to identify with the society—they must feel that they belong to it and that it belongs to them. When there are shared values, it is possible for the group to engage in common goal setting. Working toward those common goals provides another strong force in building cohesiveness. Richard C. Remy reminds us that the building of values essential to citizenship has concerned scholars and policy makers for a long time:

> Napoleon is said to have remarked that, "as long as children are not taught whether they ought to be Republican or Monarchist, Catholic or irreligious, the State will not form a Nation." Napoleon's comment reflects the fact that throughout history in both political theory and practice scholars and policy-makers have evidenced a substantial preoccupation with the political learning of the young. Plato's *Republic*, for example, devoted considerable attention to the role of education and childhood experience in the development of citizenship values. Aristotle concerned himself with "the type of

character appropriate to a constitution." Such a concern for the relationship of the state and its citizens has been continuous for most philosophers. It has been an evident theme of Hobbes, Locke, Mill, de Tocqueville, Dewey, and others.[6]

There are well-established procedures that societies use to instill and maintain these general values in their citizens. Much of this learning may not on the surface appear to have any practical or useful value. For example, the participation of schoolchildren in certain games and festivals may appear to be taking time away from other activities that have to do with "real" education. Yet societies all over the world not only allow but expect that children will participate in these activities. Indeed, an event may be perceived to be of such importance that a national holiday is declared to ensure that a proper recognition is made of it. Accordingly, children do not have to attend school on days that are so designated.

Societies make a special effort to ensure that young children learn the myths and symbols that are associated with general values and that they participate in rituals that are designed to teach them. Certain ceremonial procedures are devised for this purpose, the most obvious being the flag salute, standing at attention while the national anthem is being played or sung, displaying the flag on national holidays, and marching in ceremonial parades. These myths, symbols, and ceremonial procedures focus on outstanding achievements of the society and are designed to stress unity. Their effect is to create an awareness or a consciousness of membership and attachment to the group.

A broad spectrum of activities are used by parents, communities, and schools to achieve the purposes of value education. Parents teach the child what is expected of "good" boys and girls. They present, in one form or another, many examples of modeling behavior for the child to emulate. They use some form of punishment when behavior violates basic values. In school, children study the history of the Nation with particular attention to those cultural ideals that inspired it. Formal instruction also focuses on outstanding individuals whose lives are particularly good examples of the values the society likes to see in its citizens. Likewise, the legal and justice systems are studied because they reflect the values of the society in action.

Community life provides a constant reminder of these values. This can be observed in the deference accorded elderly persons as a matter of common courtesy or as an example of consideration for others. People respect the person and property of others. They convey greetings of good wishes or good will to each other. Communities provide displays and other reminders of values associated with ceremonial occasions. These are but a few examples of the myriad ways societies instill unifying values in their people.

What is basic?

Criterion 2:
   In the social studies those values, skills, processes, experiences, or subject matter can be considered *basic* if they develop the learners' commitment to shared, general values.

Possible subject matter and/or learning experiences
Subject matter:
1. Biographies of Americans whose lives reflect the values and ideals of the Nation.
2. Cross-cultural, comparative studies focusing on values.
3. Sources of the American heritage.
4. The ideals and principles of American democracy.
5. Ethnic heritage studies.
6. The Constitution and the Bill of Rights.
7. Landmark court decisions that highlight basic American values.

Learning experiences:
1. Analyzing American history and studying the external wellsprings of the Nation's basic values.
2. Learning the basic human rights guaranteed to all Americans regardless of race, color, creed, or national origin.
3. Studying the meaning of loyalty.
4. Engaging in role playing or simulations that illustrate value conflicts and attempting to resolve them.

Axiom 3. *Human beings spend much of their time in groups with other individuals who interact with each other according to some pattern of social organization.*

From birth to death, human beings engage in a constant stream of encounters with other human beings. These contacts with others may take a variety of forms. Some are informal, unorganized, and temporary, as for example contact with others in a crowd at a baseball game or in sharing an elevator. Other contacts are with persons in closely knit relationships of long standing, such as families and friendship groups. Still others are based on a formal membership, such as in a club, association, or an employment team. In any case, although persons are individuals, not many live their lives in isolation from others. They must associate themselves with others in order to meet their physical, psychological, and emotional needs.

Except for the most informal and transitory aggregates of people, individuals interact in groups according to a pattern of social organization. The elements of this social organization consist of roles, norms, social control, and the ranking of individuals on some criteria of preference. One does not conduct one's self in just any way one pleases in a group without running the risk of sanctions. What ordinarily happens is that the individual "knows his or her place" and behaves accordingly. In time this pattern becomes institutionalized. Persons *expect* others to behave in accordance with the social organization of the group. For instance, in school classrooms pupils expect teachers to behave as teachers and pupils to act like pupils. When teachers act like pupils, there is confusion over roles and norms. If a group does not provide sufficiently strong guidelines for individual conduct, normative confusion follows, usually resulting in disorderly and disruptive behavior.

What is basic?

Criterion 3:
In the social studies those values, skills, processes, experiences, or subject matter can be considered *basic* if they develop the learners' effectiveness in functioning in a group.

Possible subject matter and/or learning experiences
Subject matter:
1. Public policy formation.
2. Human relations studies.
3. Social power—its sources; how to exercise it; how to organize for political power.

Learning experiences:
1. Participating in decision making in the classroom and in the school.
2. Working on committees, assuming various roles in small and large groups.
3. Involvement in social action projects.

4. Relating local community, state, and national concerns to the global community and vice versa.
5. Learning how the individual relates to government at all levels; how the individual influences decisions of government.
6. Learning how competing interest groups resolve differences: examples—management-labor; environmentalists-sportsmen (or business interests); government officials-petitioners; land developers-local homeowners; and so forth.
7. Conducting an inquiry on a problem of interest.

Axiom 4. *Decision making at all levels is diffused, with vast opportunities for individual participation.*

There was a time when people were willing to elect their officals and provide those officials with the "consent to govern." Dan W. Dodson suggests that in this era of participatory democracy, people no longer give their complete consent—like a blank check—to those in authority over them.[7] As a minimum, they want and expect to monitor the actions of elected officials and also want to be included in the decision-making processes that affect them. It is a common practice today for elected officials to poll their constituents in order to get their views on particularly sensitive issues. A type of "do-it-yourself," populist attitude, along with an underlying feeling of suspicion and mistrust of officials and experts, is widespread. This is particularly apparent in social action issues dealing with the environment, urban redevelopment, school management, regulation of business practices, consumer affairs, and similar issues.

This axiom concerns itself with what Robert F. Lyke has characterized in a different context as a conflict between "substantive and procedural values in policy-formation."[8] Individuals are not likely to afford legitimacy to decisions if they have not been a party to them, no matter how sound they may be from a substantive standpoint. Unless the decision-making *procedure* involves them, the decision and the decision makers will lack credibility. Quite clearly, procedural values are given a higher priority than are substantive values when it comes to policy formation decisions. Some might argue that this may be a mistake in the long run, but those committed to the democratic process would not perceive it as such.

Another aspect of the growth of participatory democracy is the increased number of "Sunshine Laws" that have been passed in recent years. In most places it is no longer legal for public boards, commissions, councils, or legislatures to make decisions behind closed doors. Nor is it permissible to keep the records of such deliberations a secret. Public business must be conducted out in the open where any citizen can see and hear what is going on and can, if he or she chooses, contribute his or her "two-cents' worth."

What is basic?

Criterion 4:
In the social studies those values, skills, processes, experiences, or subject matter can be considered *basic* if they increase the learners' capacity to engage in decision making at all levels.

Possible subject matter and/or learning experiences
Subject matter:
1. Landmark court decisions.
2. The effects of science on social affairs at the local, state, national, and international levels.
3. The history of civil rights legislation to illustrate the role of citizen participation in social movements and policy formation.

Learning experiences:
1. Participating in decision making in the classroom and in the school.
2. Participating in group discussions.
3. Conducting inquiries: defining and identifying problems; forming and testing hypotheses; drawing conclusions based on information; analyzing and synthesizing data; distinguishing between fact and opinion; recognizing bias and propaganda; sensing cause and effect relationships; comparing and contrasting differing points of view.
4. Recognizing the value components in decision making.
5. Involvement in social action projects.

Axiom 5. *All societies need legitimate systems of social control; those who are controlled accept the legitimacy of the authority of those who govern, consider sanctions meaningful, and subscribe to the norms that regulate individual and group behavior.*

This axiom addresses itself only to social control as a basic requirement of all societies. It does not say anything about personal or individual freedom because that is not an essential requirement of a society. There are many societies throughout the world that provide very little in the way of individual freedom for their members. All of them, however, have systems of social control because it is essential to the life of the society. It just happens that individual freedom is a value highly prized by citizens of the United States. To argue that social control is not necessary because it interferes with our individual freedoms, which are constitutionally guaranteed, is absurd.

The American tradition places high value on both individual freedom *and* social order. Because these are conflicting values, one is constantly being threatened by the other. An excess of individual freedom leads to social disorder; an overzealous concern for social order erodes personal freedom. The relationship between these two concepts is often not well understood.

Societies discovered long ago that the most effective way to secure social control is to convince individual members that they should willingly comply with established norms. Basically, this is what all of education seeks to do, whether it takes place in the family, the church, the community, or in the school. Ruth Benedict's classic statement on this process of internalizing values that guide behavior says it best:

> By the time he can talk, he is the little creature of his culture, and by the time he is grown and able to take part in its activities, its habits are his habits, its beliefs are his beliefs, its impossibilities are his impossibilities.[9]

Of course, there are always those who will not comply willingly and, for this reason, societies institute law-enforcement agencies. Such nonconformists would, of necessity, be relatively few in number or the society could not survive in its present form. The consequences of widespread noncompliance would lead to a revolution. But if the general social health of the society is good, those few who do not submit voluntarily to rules and regulations do so either because of ineffective socialization or for pathological reasons.

As has already been noted, societies get individuals to behave willingly in accordance with society's requirements through the process of education. At early ages this process would more appropriately be called indoctrination, rather than education. As children grow older, however, much of this instruction should take the form of rational inquiry. The essential point here is that all societies, including our own, can and do shape the behavior of individuals in ways that make individuals feel uncomfortable when their behavior does not comply with what the society expects. This forms the basis of knowing and behaving in accordance with what is perceived as right and wrong and, of course, is fundamental to the formation of what we call a conscience.

The requirement of social order in a society should not be interpreted to mean that everyone is forced to act like everyone else or conform to a single approved lifestyle. Far from it. Most societies, and ours in particular, permit and even encourage a wide range of deviation in individual behavior. Our present emphasis on cultural and ethnic pluralism is a case in point. This simply means that the acceptable limits have been broadened, not that they do not exist at all.

What is basic?

Criterion 5:
In the social studies those values, skills, processes, experiences, or subject matter can be considered *basic* if they develop the learners' willingness to live according to the norms that govern individual and group behavior.

Possible subject matter and/or learning experiences
Subject matter:
1. Culture-bearing institutions such as the family, school, community, church, trade unions, fraternal associations, etc.
2. The law and justice systems.
3. Biographies of Americans whose lives reflect the ideals of the Nation.
4. Cross-cultural, comparative studies.
5. The meaning of civilization and its development.
6. American mores; studies of moral and ethical behavior.
7. The Constitution and the Bill of Rights.

Learning experiences:
1. Social skills such as living and working together, taking turns, respecting the rights of others, being socially sensitive, learning self-control and self-direction.
2. Analyzing current affairs and/or contemporary problems.
3. Becoming involved in legally sanctioned procedures to promote social changes in the school and community.

Axiom 6. *Societies engage in activities that are essential for societal continuity.*

A social system cannot survive with inadequate institutions to sustain fundamental aspects of human living. Social scientists find these primary activities to be universally characteristic of human societies: (1) producing goods and services; (2) distributing goods and services; (3) transporting goods and services; (4) consuming or using goods and services; (5) communicating with others; (6) protecting and conserving human and natural resources; (7) expressing aesthetic and religious impulses; (8) providing for education; (9) providing for recreation; (10) providing for government. Readers familiar with the history of social studies curriculum development will recognize that these social functions have been widely used as the basis for the social studies programs of this Nation.

A society organizes itself in ways that will make it possible for these social functions to take place in an orderly, predictable way. Steps will also be taken to ensure that skills and knowledge needed to perform them are transmitted from older to younger members. Society itself is an integrative system. It establishes mechanisms that permit individuals and groups to work and act together harmoniously in carrying out these essential social functions. It coordinates the activities of the many diverse subgroups that are a part of it.

Societies take deliberate action to ensure a strong commitment to continuity. This is one reason why school curriculums are difficult to reform and why people are apprehensive about innovations in school programs. A commitment to continuity is achieved through the use of ceremonies and rituals as well as through educational experiences and activities designed to engender affective attachment. The development of an elaborate educational system is an example of the extent to which a society will invest its resources in order to ensure continuity. Graduations, commencement exercises, retirements, anniversary celebrations, weddings, funerals, christenings, and a variety of other ceremonies and rituals associated with traditions and their maintenance are directed toward the development of attitudes of societal continuity.

What is basic?

Criterion 6:
In the social studies those values, skills, processes, experiences, or subject matter can be considered *basic* if they

field was philosophy, expressed many of his ideas about education in psychological terms. Educational psychology, particularly as it focuses on the individual learner, has profoundly affected teacher education programs in such areas as learning theory, understanding child growth and development, testing and measuring the outcomes of instruction as well as the ability to learn, personality variables and their effect on learning, teaching strategies, using materials of instruction, cultural differences and their effect on learning, and just about everything else associated with the teaching and learning process.

There are good reasons why this should be so. The objects of schooling are the learners and, therefore, the more teachers know about children and adolescents, how they grow and develop, how they are motivated, how they learn, and so on, the more effectively they can teach them. It makes sense to know something about learners' capabilities for learning, and test and measurement procedures can supply these data. Likewise, after the instruction takes place, one should evaluate to see what the effects of instruction have been. These ideas are widely accepted today—so much so that the sequence of (1) child growth and development, (2) human learning, and (3) tests and measurements (i.e. evaluation) have been institutionalized in accreditation standards for teacher education institutions, even though the labels used to describe these requirements may not be the ones used here. Additionally, methods courses and even field experiences of interns and student teachers lean heavily on concepts from educational psychology. Many of the professional textbooks used for these courses and field experiences have been authored by persons with strong backgrounds in educational psychology. The use of such terms as reinforcement, contingency schedules, establishing set, advance organizers, base-line behavior, and motivation are part of the everyday language of teacher educators and to some extent of teachers themselves. So pervasive have been the influences of educational psychology that much of the thinking relating to the present emphasis on competency based education—even this document—reflects it.

It seems apparent that this emphasis has resulted in the rise of a cult of individual psychology that often overlooks the fact that most human activities take place in social settings. It also ignores the fact that public education is designed to serve public purposes rather than private ones. Although it is true that individuals derive enormous personal benefits from their educations, this is basically not why this or any other society creates institutions called schools. The public school serves the general welfare; and, if it did not, the public would not support it with its tax revenues nor would it pass compulsory attendance laws. Undoubtedly much of the criticism of schools and school practices derives from the fact that parents and patrons do not perceive the schools as serving valued public purposes.

Competency based teacher education presupposes explicit educational goals. Indeed, it is often argued that competencies assumed necessary to effective teaching should be derived from what we want learners to know, be able to do, or feel as a result of teaching. The author suggests that the competencies of social studies teachers should be derived in part from an analysis of the basics of social studies and that teacher preparation programs should focus on the development of these competencies to a greater extent than is presently done.

In order to prepare teachers to teach the basics of social studies education, prospective teachers need heavier loadings of work in the study of society and group life than most of them get today. They need to have an understanding of how societies socialize young people and what the role of the school is in that socialization process. This may be less necessary for language teachers or those who teach mathematics, physics, or chemistry. But *all* social studies teachers and *all* elementary school teachers must be students of society. The socializing of young people for life in society is their stock in trade.

This Nation spends something in the vicinity of *96 billion* dollars each year on military expenditures because it is feared that we must keep pace with potential adversaries. To do something significantly less would presumably place our survival as a society in a position of vulnerability. What we should realize is that our survival becomes just as vulnerable—or even more so—if we fail to develop in our young people a deep commitment to the ideals, values, and lifeways of the Nation. This author knows of no society that does not take this task as a serious social responsibility. When social studies teachers and educators talk about what is basic to their field, therefore, their attention should properly focus on *survival*. If we cannot maintain ourselves as a society, nothing else really matters.

In closing, it is instructive to recall those powerful and profound thoughts of Thomas Jefferson expressed at the time of the founding of the Republic:

> I think by far the most important bill in our whole code is that for the diffusion of knowledge among the people.

> Establish the law for educating the common people. This it is the business of the state to effect.

If a nation expects to be ignorant and free, it expects what never was and never will be.

Enlighten the people generally and tyranny and oppression will vanish like evil spirits at the dawn of day.

Footnotes

[1] B. Othanel Smith and Donald E. Orlosky, *Socialization and Schooling: The Basics of Reform* (Bloomington, Indiana: Phi Delta Kappa, Inc., 1975), p. 66.

[2] Barry K. Beyer, "Teaching Basics in Social Studies," *Social Education* 41 (February 1977), pp. 96–104.

[3] Randall Collins, "Some Comparative Principles of Educational Stratification," *Harvard Educational Review* 47 (February 1977), p. 1.

[4] John Dewey, *Democracy and Education* (New York: Macmillan Publishing Co., Inc., 1916), p. 3.

[5] Jerome S. Bruner, "Some Elements of Discovery," reprinted in *Inquiry in the Social Studies*, Rodney F. Allen, John V. Fleckenstein and Peter M. Lyon, eds. (Washington, D.C.: National Council for the Social Studies, 1968), p. 15.

[6] Richard C. Remy, "Promoting Citizen Competence," *Quarterly Report* 2 (Winter 1977, Mershon Center, The Ohio State University, Columbus, Ohio), p. 1.

[7] Dan W. Dodson, "Authority, Power, and Education," *Education for an Open Society*, 1974 Yearbook, Association for Supervision and Curriculum Development, Delmo Della-Dora and James E. House, eds. (Washington, D.C.: The Association, 1974), p. 102.

[8] Robert F. Lyke, "Political Issues in School Decentralization," reprinted in *Challenges to Education: Readings for Analysis of Major Issues*, Emanuel Hurwitz, Jr. and Charles A. Tesconi, Jr., eds. (New York: Dodd, Mead & Company, 1973), p. 169.

[9] Ruth Benedict, *Patterns of Culture* (Boston: Houghton Mifflin Company, 1934), pp. 2–3.

Part Two

CBTE: Definition and Example

CBTE aggregated several accepted educational theories and practices into a comprehensive approach to teacher preparation. Consequently, there are those who claim that there is really nothing new about CBTE. They argue that when its new label is stripped away, CBTE is nothing more than "old wine in new bottles."

Those who see CBTE as a major force for the professionalization of teaching argue that it directly confronts some of the major problems associated with the establishment of full professional status for teaching. They believe it could move the profession toward development of a valid body of knowledge and repertoire of behaviors universally accepted as associated with the practice of effective teaching. It could also lead the way toward the establishment of agreed upon standards for admission to and continuance within the profession.

In Chapter 3, Loye Y. Hollis explains the basic concepts of CBTE and traces its history as a movement in the education of teachers. In the next chapter, Carl E. Schomburg describes the CBTE program used to prepare social studies teachers at the University of Houston.

Readers must form their own opinions regarding the uniqueness of CBTE. Whether its features are "new" is certainly not as important as whether it demonstrates the capacity to prepare effective teachers. Time will tell whether the movement realizes the potential many hope for it in relation to the professionalization of teaching.

3 Competency Based Teacher Education: Past, Present and Future

Loye Y. Hollis

Competency based education (CBE) is probably the most significant educational movement of this decade. Rarely, if ever, has any movement in education received as much attention. CBE has received a wide array of support and criticism. Its proponents view it as the solution to many of the critical problems and issues that face education and laud it as a response to the educational needs of today and the future. Those who oppose CBE view it as "old wine in new bottles" or as constraining and dehumanizing. They fear that CBE will reduce the goals of education to those that can be easily measured; that goals selected will be unimportant or less important than others. They believe the process of education will become mechanized to an extent that the social values in education will be reduced or lost.

There is validity in the statements made by both the proponents and opponents of CBE. Evidence can be found to support both points of view. In reality, however, the movement is too young for any conclusive judgments to be made at this time. Consequently, this chapter will not present a case for or against CBE. Furthermore, while this volume is directed toward examining competency based teacher education in relation to social studies education, no effort will be made to focus specifically on the preparation of social studies teachers in this chapter. Rather, the focus will be on providing a backdrop or perspective for viewing competency based teacher education by presenting its historical context, providing a definition and description, and exploring the present status and future prospects of the movement.

Historical Context

Competency based teacher education, as the name implies, is CBE applied to the education of teachers. Actually, the movement began as CBTE and expanded to include programs other than those for preparing teachers. Thus, in order to present the historical perspective of the movement, it is necessary to examine CBTE and its origins.

CBTE and Performance-Based Teacher Education (PBTE) are terms that are used interchangeably. According to Elam, "Probably the roots of PBTE lie in general societal conditions and the institutional responses to them characteristic of the sixties."[1] Among the most noted were (1) a heightened awareness of minority groups within the society; (2) an increased concern about the relevance of what was being taught in the schools; (3) technological advances in transportation and communication; (4) developments in the social and behavioral sciences; (5) the maturing of the education profession; (6) research and development efforts related to instruction and learning; and (7) the increased involvement of the federal government in education.

During the sixties, the rate of progress being made toward improving opportunities for minority groups was a major social concern. It was widely believed that public education was the avenue to solve most of the social "ills" of the time. Public schools were being pressed, and in some cases ordered, to attend to the problems and needs of minority children. Related to this concern, teacher education was criticized for not preparing teachers to deal with the "Real World."

Students began questioning openly the relevance of their education during the sixties. Marches, strikes, sit-ins, and other forms of confrontation were experienced on many campuses. Students expected and were demanding educational programs and opportunities that were more responsive to their needs. The crux of the problem was probably best expressed by Alvin Toffler:

> Yet for all this rhetoric about the future, our schools face backward toward a dying system, rather than forward to the emerging new society. Their vast energies are applied to cranking out Industrial Man—people tooled for survival in a system that will be dead before they are.[2]

The public demanded their schools to respond more effectively to societal and individual needs. There was almost a public mandate to change education. Society was ready and the stage was set for educational innovations. CBTE became the primary response and innovation of teacher preparation programs.

Technology was advancing and expanding at a rapid rate. Miniaturization and mass production made television, tape recorders, calculators, and other devices available to almost everyone. Teachers had a new arsenal of equipment at their disposal. Some of what they had done in the past could now be done by a machine and, in some cases, done better. The role of the teacher was beginning to change from that of a disseminator of information to a facilitator of learning. And, for the first time in our history, the technology was available to implement this approach to education.

Coupled with social and technological advances were advances in the behavioral and social sciences. According to Hall and Jones, three theoretical developments were essential predecessors of the emergence of CBTE:

1. The reversal of educational practice away from group instruction and group comparisons toward emphasis on the individual as the controller of his own learning.
2. The concept of mastery learning.
3. The redefinition of "aptitude."[3]

Hall and Jones stated, "the trend away from grouped instruction and comparisons of individual achievement against group curves quite likely found its impetus in a reaction against the gray-flannel-suit regimentation and button-down minds of the fifties and sixties."[4] Concerns of society about the acceptance and development of each person's unique characteristics caused schools to seek new modes of instruction, modes that made it possible to respond to the individual.

Many educators believed the application of the concept of mastery learning would solve the individualization problem. The basic premise of mastery learning as stated by Bloom is, "Most students (perhaps more than 90 per cent) can master what we have to teach them, and it is the task of instruction to find the means which will enable them to master the subject under consideration."[5] Bloom's position is rather clear. Students can learn and it is the teacher's responsibility to provide an environment and process in which they can learn. His position is supported by Carroll, who suggested that aptitude is the amount of time required by the learner to attain mastery of a learning task. This is in stark contrast to the assumption that some students can learn and others cannot. If Carroll's assumption is correct, then educational programs should be designed to allow each student the amount of time needed to master the subject under consideration. These concepts exerted a powerful influence on the development of CBTE.

The education profession was beginning to make its presence more evident during the sixties. Teacher organizations became stronger and more vocal in insisting that they have an increased and more important role in educational decisions. Teacher organizations adopted many of the practices of labor unions. And, as a group, they were being recognized as a strong political body and were accomplishing many of their objectives. As salaries were being improved, school boards began wanting evidence of productivity. CBTE, with its precise objectives and mastery learning concepts, seemed a logical response.

Research and development in instruction and learning were opening new educational avenues. New programs were being developed and implemented in the schools. Individually Guided Instruction (IGI), Individually Prescribed Instruction (IPI), and Computer Assisted Instruction (CAI) are examples of such approaches. These programs were designed for individuals, not groups. Each of these approaches involved stating specifically what was to be learned. This is one of the essential elements in CBTE programs. The work of Flanders and others with interaction analysis systems provided an additional means for studying instruction and learning. The educational process could be studied in ways previously not possible. The performance of both teacher and learners could be recorded, analyzed, and evaluated. This was a necessary prerequisite for the development of performance based education programs.

The federal role in education had been accepted and recognized. Funding of National Science Foundation Programs following Sputnik had legitimized their intervention in public education. This was followed by the funding of Research and Development Centers, the Bureau of Educational Personnel Development Task Force 72, the Models Project, Teacher Corps projects, Training Teachers of Teachers projects, Elementary Teacher Education, and the Multi-State Consortium of Performance Based Teacher Education. Thus, the heavy influx of federal dollars made it possible to conceptualize and develop new approaches to the preparation of teachers.

According to Steffenson, "The major impetus for CBTE may be traced back to late 1967 when the Bureau of Research within the Office of Education issued a request for proposals to support the development" of specifications for a comprehensive program for the preparation of undergraduate and inservice teachers.[6] In 1968 ten teacher education institutions were funded by the Office of Education to design model elementary teacher education programs. The Models Project, according to Steffenson, "is generally identified as providing the early literature associated with competency based teacher education."[7]

Following the completion of the Models Project, Teacher Corps Programs and Training Teachers of Teachers' (TTT) Programs began emphasizing CBTE. They provided much of the thrust and incentive for institutions to implement CBTE. Steffenson notes, "the National Center for Improvement of Educational Systems and Teacher Corps are viewed as being the OE programs most persistently involved with the exploration of CBTE as a system through which the restructuring of teacher education might take place."[8]

During this time professional organizations became interested in CBTE. The American Association of Colleges for Teacher Education (AACTE) established a committee on Performance Based Teacher Education. This organization has been a continuing source of ideas and materials for CBTE.

The conditions that were present in the sixties set the stage for the CBTE movement. CBTE was not so much a reaction to the educational practices and conditions of the past as it was a response to the educational needs of that time and perceived needs of the future. This belief was stated by Howsam and Houston:

> In changing times, unchanging schools are anomalous. Competency based education promises the thrust necessary for adaption to meet the challenge of a changed and changing society.... The emphasis in competency based teacher education on objectives, accountability, and personalization implies specific criteria, careful evaluation, change based on feedback, and relevant programs for a modern era.[9]

Definition and Description

Two basic principles govern competency based education: (1) teaching and/or learning become more effective and efficient when the learner understands what is expected or required, and (2) teaching and/or learning become effective and efficient when the learner's rate and mode of learning are varied according to his/her aptitude and interest. These basic principles are those embraced by mastery learning.

The most widely quoted and accepted definition of CBTE was presented by Stanley Elam in *Performance Based Teacher Education: What Is the State of the Art?* In August 1971, the AACTE committee sponsored a conference in which experts discussed the salient aspects of CBE. Elam's report was a synthesis of their deliberations. This report identified the essential characteristics which are listed below:

1. Competencies (knowledge, skills, behaviors) to be demonstrated by the student are:
   —derived from explicit conceptions of teacher roles.
   —stated so as to make possible assessment of a student's behavior in relation to specific competencies.
   —made public in advance.
2. Criteria to be employed in assessing competencies are:
   —based upon, and in harmony with, specified competencies.
   —explicit in stating expected levels of mastery under specified conditions.
   —made public in advance.
3. Assessment of the student's competency:
   —uses his performance as the primary source of evidence.
   —takes into account evidence of the student's knowledge relevant to planning for, analyzing, interpreting, or evaluating situations or behavior.
   —strives for objectivity.
4. The student's rate of progress through the program is determined by demonstrated competency rather than by time or course completion.
5. The instructional program is intended to facilitate the development and evaluation of the student's achievement of competencies specified.[10]

An additional view of CBTE may be useful in understanding the concept. Houston and Howsam summarize their position:

> Competency based instruction is a simple, straightforward concept with the following central characteristics: (a) specification of learner objectives in behavioral terms; (b) specification of the means for determining whether performance meets the indicated criterion levels; (c) provision for one or more modes of instruction pertinent to the objectives, through which the learning activities may take place; (d) public sharing of the objectives, criteria, means of assessment, and alternative activities; (e) assessment of the learning experience in terms of competency criteria; and (f) placement on the learner of the accountability for meeting the criteria. Other concepts and procedures—such as modularized packaging, the systems approach, educational technology, and guidance and management support—are employed as means in implementing the competency based commitment. For the most part, these contributory concepts are related to individualization.[11]

An analysis of the definitions of CBTE yields a rather simple and uncomplicated process. The intent is clear:

1. Specify and require the knowledge, skills, behaviors, and attitudes that are expected of teachers.

2. Communicate specifically what is required.
3. Facilitate the completion of the requirement and make allowances in learning mode and in time for completion.
4. Evaluate and make the learner accountable for what was initially communicated.

The single most important characteristic of a competency based program is the competencies to be demonstrated by the learners. Specification of competencies is a crucial aspect of designing the instructional program. Cooper, Jones, and Weber assert there are four different bases from which statements of teacher competencies can be generated: philosophical, empirical, subject matter, and practitioner.[12]

The philosophical approach to selecting competencies is based upon identification and acceptance of a set of assumptions about the nature of human beings and society, the purpose of education, and the nature of learning and instruction. Assumptions are hypotheses that are expressions of beliefs or values that may or may not have been validated. Assumptions are used by CBTE designers as the basis for specifying competencies that describe the "ideal" teacher. For example, if the ability to individualize instruction is valued as a teaching skill of the "ideal" teacher, then the competencies specified would likely include the ability to diagnose, prescribe, and implement the prescription. Thus, if designers value a model of a teacher that employs the clinical approach to teaching, assumptions regarding that role model can be developed and competencies derived from those assumptions.

An empirical approach to selecting competencies relies on what is known about teaching and learning. Teaching skills such as positive reinforcement, providing immediate feedback, set induction, and stimulus variation would be included in the list of competencies. Data from research form the basis for the specification of competencies. Obviously, one difficulty with this approach is that not enough is known about what behaviors are related to effective and ineffective teaching.

The subject-matter approach uses what the teacher needs to know and be able to do in the content areas he/she is expected to teach. Curriculum guides and textbooks that are being used in the schools form the prime source for determining the competencies that are required. This approach requires the analysis of what elementary and secondary students are expected to learn. The knowledge explosion and the rate at which content changes in the schools present obvious problems when using this approach.

A practitioner approach requires an analysis of what teachers do in the classroom. Competency statements are based on the observed behavior of teachers. Competencies derived in this fashion have face validity because successful teachers demonstrate these behaviors. However, this approach tends to promote the status quo and often limits programs to the present. There is a danger that competencies needed in the future might not be considered.

A fifth approach, course translation, is probably the most commonly used by teacher educators. Competency statements are specified by using the requirements of existing courses. The total set of competencies derived from the courses constitutes the program. One very obvious flaw in this approach is that it does not eliminate the gaps and overlaps that may exist in the program. In addition, the set of competencies that are specified may not adequately contain all that are needed by teachers.

Most authorities recommend that program developers use no single approach when specifying competencies. All five can be used, thus eliminating or at least reducing the deficiencies that may exist when any one approach is employed. One approach is normally used to generate an initial set of competency statements and the other approaches are used to expand and refine the set.

The major problem that exists with competency specification is pure and simple fact: *We do not know what competencies are essential for effective teaching.* As stated by Dodl:

> Probably the most persistent and pervasive problem facing CBTE is charges by both critics and supporters that the selected competencies have no validity. Competency validity basically means acceptable evidence exists that possession of a competency or set of competencies "makes a difference." Teachers with a given set of competencies bring about the intended performance results of specific teaching functions.[13]

Recognizing where we are with respect to the study of teaching and its effectiveness, a competency statement should be considered a hypothesis to be studied and tested. As such, competency statements are likely to change or be modified when more is known about teaching and learning. Competency statements should reflect what is known and believed about teaching and learning at any given point in time, and they should be viewed as increasing opportunities for examination and study of teaching effectiveness.

Five types of competencies are normally specified in CBTE programs:

1. Cognitive competencies which specify what the teacher is expected to know. They result from addressing the question: What should a teacher know in order to be effective?
2. Performance competencies which specify the behaviors the teacher is expected to demonstrate. They result from the question: What should a teacher be able to do in order to be effective?
3. Consequence competencies which specify what changes the teacher will cause to occur in others. They result from the question: What changes would an effective teacher produce in others?
4. Affective competencies which specify the attitudes the teacher is expected to demonstrate. They result from the question: What beliefs, values, interests, appreciations, and feelings are characteristic of an effective teacher?
5. Exploratory competencies which specify an event in which the teacher is expected to participate. They result from the question: What experiences might be helpful to the development of an effective teacher?

Most CBTE programs will employ all five types; however, stronger emphasis is usually placed on performance, consequence, and affective competencies.

A distinction should be made between a goal and a competency. A goal is a statement of program intent. The statement, "to produce an effective teacher of social studies," is an example of a goal. The statement, "The teacher will use an inquiry strategy effectively and appropriately when teaching a social studies lesson," is an example of a competency. Goals focus the program while competencies focus the learner. Consequently, competencies are derived from goals. The set of competencies specified for a given goal should clearly communicate what is required of the learner to achieve the goal.

Since competency statements are normally broad and inclusive, it is usually necessary to delineate them further by specifying and sequencing instructional objectives. Program designers usually employ four types of instructional objectives: cognitive, performance, consequence, and affective. They are derived from competencies and specify the abilities and/or attitudes needed for demonstration of the competency. The comprehensiveness of the competency statement will determine the number of instructional objectives students may need to achieve in order to acquire the competency. Figure 1 illustrates the relationship between goals, competencies, and objectives.[14]

Figure 1
SPECIFYING INSTRUCTIONAL INTENT

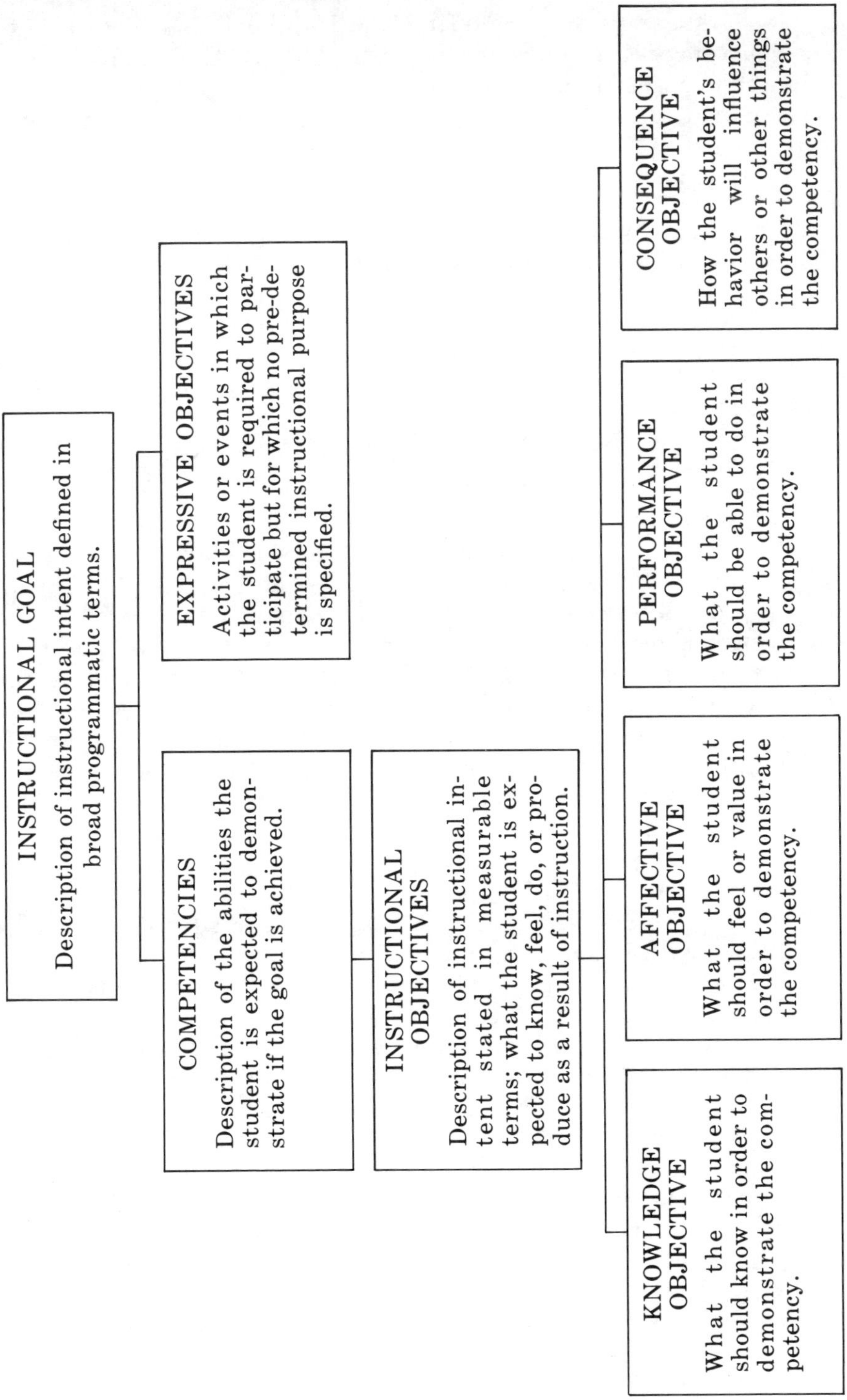

INSTRUCTIONAL GOAL
Description of instructional intent defined in broad programmatic terms.

COMPETENCIES
Description of the abilities the student is expected to demonstrate if the goal is achieved.

EXPRESSIVE OBJECTIVES
Activities or events in which the student is required to participate but for which no pre-determined instructional purpose is specified.

INSTRUCTIONAL OBJECTIVES
Description of instructional intent stated in measurable terms; what the student is expected to know, feel, do, or produce as a result of instruction.

KNOWLEDGE OBJECTIVE
What the student should know in order to demonstrate the competency.

AFFECTIVE OBJECTIVE
What the student should feel or value in order to demonstrate the competency.

PERFORMANCE OBJECTIVE
What the student should be able to do in order to demonstrate the competency.

CONSEQUENCE OBJECTIVE
How the student's behavior will influence others or other things in order to demonstrate the competency.

Assessment of instructional objectives as well as competencies is implicit in the concept of CBTE. Equally implicit is that assessment will be criterion referenced, not norm referenced, and that assessment criteria and procedures will be made public to students in advance of instruction. As noted by Airasian:

> As various authors concerned with performance-based teacher education have indicated, criterion-referenced as opposed to norm-referenced evaluation is needed. With respect to each required competency, we will want to know whether the student has achieved criterion-level performance, not how high or low he stands relative to other students. Criterion-referenced evaluation, which many argue is more relevant, humane, and "fair" than norm-referenced evaluation, is possible only when criterion performance is predefined.[15]

Simply stated, the learner knows what will be assessed, how it will be assessed, and the standard of achievement that is required to master the competency or objective.

There seems to be common agreement that one of the knottiest problems in CBTE is the assessment of competency attainment. According to Hall and Jones, "Friend and foe agree, a major problem in competency-based education is assessment of the acquisition of competency."[16] Ward, Morine, and Berliner stated, "We do not as yet know enough about which aspects of teaching are essential for affecting student performance positively to use specific levels of teaching performance as 'go' or 'no go' criteria for entry into or promotion within the profession."[17]

CBTE program developers are aware of the problems associated with evaluation. Since students are held accountable for demonstrating specified competencies, not for how they attain them, judgments regarding progression through and exiting must be based on valid and reliable data. It is crucial, therefore, that evaluation procedures employed be the best that are available and continually improved.

Instructional activities are usually provided to assist students in meeting objectives. Theoretically, students are free to choose learning activities most suited to their needs and interests. Most authorities recommend the use of instructional modules in CBTE programs. As stated by Cooper and Weber:

> At the very heart of the competency based teacher education program is the instructional module. An instructional module can be defined as a set of learning activities intended to facilitate the

PROFESSIONALIZING SOCIAL STUDIES TEACHING

learner's acquisition and demonstration of a particular competency or particular competencies.[18]

Most instructional modules contain the following:

1. A rationale that describes the purpose and importance of the objectives of the module and how the objectives relate to a competency and the total program.
2. Objectives that specify what the learner is required to demonstrate.
3. Prerequisites that specify what, if anything, is required for entering the module.
4. Preassessment that (a) assesses the prerequisite requirements and (b) provides an opportunity to determine if the objectives of the module have previously been acquired.
5. Learning activities which provide various learning options for the student.
6. Post-assessment that permits the student to demonstrate achievement of the objectives.

There are several aspects of instructional modules that are worth noting:

1. They are self-paced, thereby facilitating the individualization of instruction.
2. The number of learning options that are provided to students promotes personalization of instruction.
3. They are not restrictive. Lectures, seminars, field activities, mediated materials, to mention a few, can be used as learning activities.
4. They can be designed for groups of students as well as individuals.
5. Students are provided with feedback and direction upon entry to and during the module.

Instructional modules should be viewed in the context of the total system. Many modules constitute a total program and form an instructional system. Modules are clustered and sequenced to promote effective and efficient learning. Students proceed from module to module as they demonstrate competence. Thus, they proceed through the instructional system in the same manner they proceed through a module. In essence, the program is an instructional system comprised of a set of instructional modules.

Although, in the strictest sense, it is not essential for CBTE programs to be field-centered, it is desirable and highly recommended. Most, if not all, CBTE programs provide field activities throughout the program. Demonstration of most consequence competencies/objectives requires a field context, and many performance competencies/objectives are best demonstrated in the field context. Additionally, school-based teacher educators can be invaluable in the assessment of competencies/objectives.

In summary, a CBTE program is an instructional system. It allows individuals to progress and exit as they are able to demonstrate competence. Optional learning activities are provided, thus allowing for individual differences and preferences. The program is accountable for providing effective and efficient learning and assessment activities, and the learner is accountable for the demonstration of competence. Instructional modules are recommended as the vehicle for program delivery, and field activities are highly desirable for both learning and evaluation activities.

Present Status and Future Prospects

A comparison of the results of surveys of Colleges and Universities is reported by Kay and Massanari as follows:[19]

Table 1. Growth of C/PBTE in Institutions of Higher Education Between 1972 and 1975

Category of Involvement	1972 No.	1972 %	1975 No.	1975 %
Operating limited or full-scale CBTE programs	131	17	296	52
Not Involved	228	29	98	17
Exploration or Development	424	54	176	31
Totals	783	100	570	100

This would suggest that the CBTE movement had prospered between 1972 and 1975 and that it was rather widespread in 1975.

It is difficult to assess the quality of existing CBTE programs. Roth surveyed 215 institutions that were listed as having CBTE programs and concluded that:

> Statements about CBTE effectiveness in general, or comparisons of the CBTE approach with other approaches, cannot be made in the

absence of a generally accepted definition of CBTE and a number of operational programs whose design is consistent with such a definition.[20]

The main problem in evaluating CBTE seems to be that the program assumptions, goals, and competencies differ among the programs. This results in programs with different operational procedures and products. Additionally, it takes several years to conceptualize and operationalize a program, and several additional years are needed before their products begin teaching. This fact, coupled with the inadequacy of our teaching effectiveness measures, makes a valid evaluation of CBTE impossible at this time.

A survey of states regarding performance-based teacher certification (PBTC) was conducted in 1972, a second in 1974, and a third in 1976. The 1976 survey was used to determine if any trends had developed since 1974.

> The results of the survey indicate that many states are continuing to increase involvement in competency based teacher education and certification. Specifically, fourteen states have identified additional activities which they were not involved in during 1974, whereas only four states have reported decreasing activities since 1974.[21]

CBTE is a controversial issue. Merrow reported that "The organized teaching profession shows no signs of supporting CBTE."[22] Arnold and others report:

> In several states (for example, Texas, New York, and Florida) regulations were established requiring teacher preparation programs to be structured in a competency mode within a certain time period. In New York, teacher organizations voiced strong opposition, holding that there were no provisions for significant teacher involvement in the planning process. In Texas, an Attorney General's ruling held that a competency mode for preparation programs represented but one alternative, with institutions being permitted to develop and implement programs organized around other rationales as well. To many, including a number of individuals strongly supportive of competency based teacher education, the movement toward mandating competency based preparation programs through certification regulations represents a serious error.[23]

Although there is opposition to CBTE, there seems to be a strong trend in that direction. Controversy exists over whether the state should specify the competencies or the institutions should specify them and have them approved by the state. Independent of who and how competencies are specified, the public seems to be viewing CBTE as a means of holding teachers and teacher preparation institutions accountable.

During 1975–76, the PBTE Project of AACTE studied CBTE as applied to inservice education. Inquiries were mailed to state departments of education, Teacher Corps staffs, colleges and universities offering CBTE pre-service programs, and teacher center directors. From the responses to the inquiry, 466 inservice programs were identified. A sample of 188 was selected for the survey; 77 responses were received. One of the summary remarks was:

> It appears that a variety of exciting and interesting activity is underway in various environments and by many people under the rubric of competency based inservice education. In a number of centers, efforts are being made to apply pieces and/or elements of a competency based approach, but it appears that there are few full-blown CBTE programs underway in the area of inservice education.[24]

The increased interest in teacher accountability has resulted in a renewed interest in CBTE. Airasian notes:

> Performance-based teacher education is here today not as the result of a ground-swell of support from teachers, but because administrators and politicians believe it is a rational, efficient, and accountable method of training and certifying teachers, as well it may be. Performance-based programs are with us because they are believed to be better by those who have some say in the matter, not because research evidence overwhelmingly indicates their superiority. The decision has proceeded from the top downwards. In short, the values implicit in a performance-based approach fit closely with the values of legislators and administrators.[25]

It is difficult, if not impossible, to make an accurate analysis of the present status of or future prospects for CBTE. Some aspects of the movement seem clear:

1. There is no standard format or set of criteria being employed when CBTE programs are implemented. What is called CBTE in one institution would not meet the standards of another and vice versa.
2. Impetus for the movement is being generated from authority figures in and outside of the Teaching Profession. The public's interest in accountability has resulted in new support.
3. The number of institutions reporting CBTE programs is in-

creasing. The rate is not as rapid as it was earlier in the movement's history. This is probably due to the reduction in external funding for CBTE program implementation.
4. The concept of CBTE is expanding to include programs other than preservice programs. Inservice programs are being designed using aspects of CBTE.

Views differ on CBTE's prospects for the future. For example, Massanari states:

> Some people believe that CBTE is just another development which will fade away into the oblivion of educational faddism. On the other hand, some of us believe that CBTE—given intelligent leadership and adequate development and research support—can generate the kinds of reform so long sought and now so urgently needed.[26]

Probably the single most critical element to CBTE's failure or success is the validation of competencies and the instrumentation and processes to measure them. CBTE is now widespread and has substantial support. Logically and theoretically, it makes sense. However, the linkage of specific teacher behaviors to desired changes in student behavior is imperative. Essential to this is the ability to measure accurately those behaviors. This will take time, commitment, collaboration, and resources.

Epilogue

CBTE was conceived during the educational upheavals of the sixties and early seventies. Conception resulted from the needs of the individual, society, and the Teaching Profession. Birth was possible because of advances in the behavioral sciences, technology, and communication.

As a young child, CBTE was criticized for being too different and for not being different enough. It was compared with its elders, and told it must justify and prove itself, even though its elders had not been and were not being required to do so.

The CBTE youth of today continues to develop and expand. As all youth, it is immature and weak. Inadequate means of competency validation, undeveloped evaluation systems, and inadequate, sometimes inappropriate, implementation are but a few of its growing pains. The disease of inappropriate use and misunderstanding is ever present and could cripple or destroy.

Prospects for maturity, as with any growing thing, depend on the environment. Our Profession, the parent, will in large measure make that decision. If we embrace and care about the principles represented by CBTE, it will continue to develop. If not, it will be abused or misused or die. The choice is ours. Let's hope it is a wise one.

Footnotes

[1] Stanley Elam, *Performance-Based Teacher Education, What Is the State of the Art?*, PBTE Series: No. 1 (Washington, D.C.: American Association of Colleges for Teacher Education, December 1971), p. 2.

[2] Alvin Toffler, *Future Shock* (New York: Random House, Inc., 1970), pp. 398–399.

[3] Gene E. Hall and Howard L. Jones, *Competency-Based Education: A Process for the Improvement of Education* (Englewood Cliffs: Prentice-Hall, Inc., 1976), p. 8.

[4] *Ibid.*

[5] Benjamin S. Bloom, J. Thomas Hastings, and George F. Madaus, "Learning for Mastery," in *Handbook on Formative and Summative Evaluation of Student Learning* (New York: McGraw-Hill, 1971), p. 43.

[6] James Steffenson, "Foreword," in *Exploring Competency Based Education*, Houston, ed., p. xiv.

[7] *Ibid.*, p. xiii.

[8] *Ibid.*, pp. xiii–xiv.

[9] W. Robert Houston and Robert B. Howsam, eds., "Change and Challenge," *Competency-Based Teacher Education: Progress, Problems, and Prospects* (Chicago: Science Research Associates, Inc., 1972), p. 1.

[10] Elam, *Performance-Based Teacher Education, What Is the State of the Art?*, pp. 6–11. (Printed with permission of A.A.C.T.E.)

[11] Houston and Howsam, *Competency-Based Teacher Education: Progress, Problems, and Prospects*, pp. 5–6.

[12] James M. Cooper, Howard L. Jones, and Wilford A. Weber, "Specifying Teacher Competencies," *Journal of Teacher Education*, Vol. XXIV, No. 1 (Spring 1973), p. 17.

[13] Norman R. Dodl, "Selecting Competency Outcomes for Teacher Education," *Journal of Teacher Education*, Vol. XXIV, No. 3 (Fall 1973), p. 197.

[14] B. Dell Felder, Classroom materials used at the Universidad Autonoma de Guadalajara, Mexico, July 5, 1977.

[15] Peter Airasian, "Performance-Based Teacher Education: Evaluation Issues," in *Performance Education Assessment*, Theodore E. Andrews, ed. (The University of the State of New York and the Multistate Consortium on Performance-Based Teacher Education), p. 17.

[16] Hall and Jones, *Competency-Based Education: A Process for the Improvement of Education*, p. 59.

[17] Beatrice Ward, Greta Morine, and David C. Berliner, "Assessing Teacher Competence," in *Competency Assessment, Research, and Evaluation: A Report of a National Conference*, W. Robert Houston, ed. (Washington, D.C.: American Association of Colleges for Teacher Education, March 12–15, 1974), p. 124.

[18] James M. Cooper and Wilford A. Weber, "A Competency Based Systems Approach to Teacher Education," in *Competency Based Teacher Education 2: A Systems Approach to Program Design*, James M. Cooper, Wilford A. Weber, and Charles E. Johnson, eds. (Berkeley: McCutchan Publishing Corporation, 1973), p. 17.

[19] Patricia M. Kay and Karl Massanari, *PBTE 1977: Where To From Here?* (Washington, D.C.: The American Association of Colleges for Teacher Education, October, 1977), p. 14.

[20] Robert A. Roth, "How Effective Are CBTE Programs?" *Phi Delta Kappan*, Vol. 58, No. 10 (June 1977), p. 760.

[21] Robert A. Roth, *Performance Based Teacher Certification 1976, A Survey of the States* (Lansing: Michigan Department of Education, 1976), p. 33.

[22] John G. G. Merrow, II, *The Politics of Competence: A Review of Competency-Based Teacher Education, A Report to the National Institute of Education* (Washington, D.C.: Institute for Educational Leadership, July 1974), p. 13.

[23] Daniel S. Arnold and others, *Quality Control in Teacher Education: Some Policy Issues* (Washington, D.C.: The American Association of Colleges for Teacher Education and the ERIC Clearinghouse on Teacher Education, May 1977), p. 43.

[24] Performance-Based Teacher Education Committee, *Report of Survey on Competency-Based Inservice Education* (Washington, D.C.: American Association of Colleges for Teacher Education, August 15, 1976).

[25] Peter Airasian, "Performance-Based Teacher Education: Evaluation Issues," *Performance Education Assessment*, p. 13.

[26] Karl Massanari, "CBTE's Potential for Improving Educational Personnel Development," *Journal of Teacher Education*, Vol. XXIV, No. 3 (Fall 1973), p. 247.

4 Integrating the Social Studies Component in a CBTE Model

Carl E. Schomburg

Theoretically, competency based teacher education (CBTE) involves specifying the competencies thought associated with effective teaching and developing means to assist students to demonstrate those competencies. One approach is to translate existing courses into the competency based mode. The difficulty with this approach is that often little attention is given to articulating the component parts of the program into a logical whole. Perhaps one course builds upon another. Perhaps the program gives attention to all aspects of teaching which seem important. Perhaps not. Program articulation may be more a matter of chance than of design.

The many different components of a CBTE program should work together to provide an effective and efficient preparation program for students. At the University of Houston an instructional system was developed in which all parts of the CBTE program are designed to work together. The social studies component of this CBTE program has been designed as an integral part of the overall teacher education model.

The University of Houston CBTE Model[1]

In designing a CBTE program, the faculty at Houston faced the difficult problem (as have all who have attempted to develop CBTE programs) of having to specify competencies in the absence of an empirical research base to support this effort. Validated knowledge of what constitutes effective teaching behaviors is very limited. For this reason, it was necessary for the faculty to take another approach to the identification of competencies. *Assumptions* about the nature of learning, the needs of society, and the role of an effective teacher were agreed upon. These assumptions formed the basis for subsequent specification of competencies. It is important to note here that faculty at Houston treat competencies as hypotheses. Competency statements represent the faculty's best "hunches" regarding those behaviors related to effective teaching. As hypotheses, however, competency statements are subject to change as additional knowledge becomes available.

The faculty decided that the most effective means for assisting students to develop desired competencies was an *instructional systems* approach to the design and delivery of the program. CBTE emphasizes the use of a systemic approach to curriculum planning and implementation. The basic assumption underlying the systemic approach is that all parts must fit together to make the whole and that changes in one component of the system (or program) cause changes in all other components of the system. This approach, it was felt, would come closest to assuring that all experiences of the prospective teacher were integrated into a meaningful whole. Further, such an approach made it more likely that constraints would be more realistically acknowledged and more carefully attended.

The specific characteristics of the CBTE instructional system were defined by the faculty through agreement to a set of assumptions regarding its operation. For example, the faculty agreed that competency statements, assessment criteria, and assessment procedures would be made public to students in advance of instruction. Further, it was agreed that students would be held accountable for the demonstration, not the *acquisition*, of competencies. Program delivery would involve the use of modules as a means of communication. The program would include both school-based and college-based experiences and would be individualized and personalized for students. These and other assumptions defined the faculty's perception of the characteristics of the most effective and efficient program for training teachers. These assumptions became, and continue to be, a powerful influence on the actual design and delivery of the competency based teacher education program at Houston.

Competencies identified for the program are either generic or specialized. Generic competencies reflect those teaching behaviors considered essential for all teachers to master if they are to be effective, regardless of subject area field or level (elementary or secondary) of preparation. Generic competencies are derived primarily from assumptions about learning, teaching, and human development. Specialized competencies describe those behaviors considered essential for effective teaching of a subject area or level. These competencies usually build upon generic competencies and are derived to a greater degree from assumptions and/or knowledge unique to particular disciplines.

Since the preservice teacher is prepared to teach social studies within the context of the larger instructional system at the University of Houston, it is important to identify the generic competencies which these students are expected to demonstrate. Social studies competencies are designed to build and extend these generic skills and to respond to the unique dimensions of social studies education.

All students preparing to teach at the University of Houston are expected to demonstrate successfully the following sixteen generic competencies. They must demonstrate the ability to:

1. Identify the learner's emotional, social, physical, and intellectual needs.
2. Identify and/or specify instructional goals and objectives which are based on learner's needs.
3. Design instruction appropriate to goals and objectives.
4. Implement instruction that is consistent with plans.
5. Design and implement evaluation procedures which focus on learner achievement and instructional effectiveness.
6. Integrate into instruction the cultural environment of students.
7. Demonstrate a repertoire of instructional models and teaching skills appropriate to specified objectives and to particular learners.
8. Promote effective patterns of communication.
9. Use resources appropriate to instructional objectives.
10. Modify instruction on the basis of learner's verbal and nonverbal feedback during instruction.
11. Use organizational and management skills to establish a maximally effective learning environment.
12. Identify and react with sensitivity to the needs and feelings of self and others.
13. Exhibit openness and flexibility.
14. Work effectively as a member of a professional team.
15. Analyze professional effectiveness and continually strive to increase that effectiveness.
16. Design and implement instruction which incorporates career education concepts.[2]

As mentioned earlier, students are held accountable for the *demonstration*, not the acquisition of competencies. Objectives and assessment criteria are made clear and public to the student in advance of instruction. Instructional modules are used to communicate objectives, assessment criteria, and learning alternatives to students.

Every effort is made to respond to the individual needs and interests of students. Learning alternatives available in the modules provide for differences in learning styles. For example, students who learn some things best through visual means might choose an alternative which has been developed around slide or film presentations. If the printed word is the most effective means for some students to learn, those students have opportunities to select learning options which contain a wide range of reading activities. If a student can determine a way of meeting the instructional objective(s) by some means not listed in a module, that becomes a negotiable item between the instructor and student. Also, if a student can demonstrate competence without attending class, he or she is permitted to do so. The student, then, is held responsible for his or her own learning. The student becomes an active participant in deciding how he or she will learn. The student must learn to make rational decisions in choosing from available alternatives and to assume responsibility for those decisions.

The program is divided into four phases. These phases are equivalent to four semesters at the Junior and Senior years. Early in their first semester, students are exposed to a variety of situations designed to help them decide whether teaching is the best professional choice for them. In Phases I and II, students spend approximately one-half of their time working in public school classrooms as observer-aides. This experience provides the student with the opportunity to see firsthand what teaching is all about. For many, it is the first time back in a classroom since they left one many years ago. This time they are observing teaching from the teacher-learner point of view. When faced with the reality of classroom teaching, some students decide that teaching is not for them or that they would be better suited to teach at another level. This may mean focusing on the intermediate level instead of the primary level or even changing from the elementary to the secondary certification program.

During Phases I and II, students are provided experiences which focus on developing generic teaching skills such as the ability to ask lower and higher order questions, set induction techniques, lesson planning, and positive reinforcement techniques. Generic teaching competencies are *re-visited* in subsequent program components, and the student is constantly called upon to demonstrate the ability to apply these skills to the teaching of various content.

Students are provided opportunities to practice their skills in both peer teaching and public school classroom situations.

Their lessons are recorded on video-tape. Faculty use these video-tapes to assist students to analyze their teaching behaviors to identify and focus on areas which need improvement.

Students are exposed to a variety of educational settings throughout the program. They observe and work in inner city and suburban schools. They visit alternative schools, and schools with special or innovative programs. A close working relationship exists between teachers in the public schools and the University faculty. Public school teachers, called School Based Teacher Educators, play an important part in the training of students. School Based Teacher Educators are carefully chosen for participation in the program and are provided continuous inservice training related to their responsibilities through a Teacher Center established for this purpose.

Integrating the Social Studies Component

During Phase III, students are expected to integrate specific methods strategies into their teaching repertoires. Social studies assumes a new meaning at this point because students must now demonstrate the ability to apply generic strategies using a social studies format. In addition, specialized competencies in social studies are introduced. Each social studies competency must be satisfactorily demonstrated before the student is allowed to enter the student teaching phase of the program.

In designing the social studies component of a CBTE program, it is necessary to identify the purpose or goal which this component is expected to serve. The obvious point of departure for designing the program is to specify purpose. What knowledge, skills and attitudes should the social studies teacher possess? What behaviors should a social studies teacher be able to foster in his or her students?

The answers to these questions determine the content of a social studies methods component in a CBTE framework. Once assumptions about an educational program have been made, goals can be developed, and competencies and objectives needed to make these goals a reality can be identified. Until this is done, there will be little or no understanding as to what type of teachers will be produced or what types of behaviors will be sought in their students. Few teacher preparation programs have followed this systemic approach; the outcome being conflicting aims resulting in confusion for all involved.

Just as assumptions were drawn for the entire CBTE pro-

PROFESSIONALIZING SOCIAL STUDIES TEACHING

gram, assumptions were also established for the social studies component. Assumptions are hypotheses that reflect value judgments about social studies that are thought to be valid, but not necessarily empirically correct. Assumptions may be drawn from two areas: (1) assumptions about how the social studies teacher and student learn best; and (2) assumptions of current and future societal needs that can be made through social studies instruction. The process of stating assumptions results in a conceptualization of the role of the teacher in the social studies classroom. Examples of assumptions that can be made for a social studies methods component are as follows:

1. Society needs social studies teachers and students who are dedicated to rational decision making if the democratic process is to function efficiently.
2. Society needs social studies teachers and students who are prepared for and actively participating in a multicultural society.
3. Society needs social studies teachers and students who are operating at a principled stage of moral development.
4. Optimal learning occurs when data are organized according to the concepts and generalizations of each social science discipline.
5. Optimal learning occurs when the teacher provides the student with a variety of instructional modes relevant to the individual needs of his students.
6. Optimal learning occurs when teachers and students learn to think critically using an inductive mode for processing social studies data.
7. Optimal learning occurs when teachers and students are encouraged to examine their own values.
8. Optimal learning occurs when the future teacher is presented with a model of the teacher he or she is expected to become.[3]

Assumptions such as these constitute the building blocks of the total social studies program. Goals are derived from the assumptions and serve as the parameters of the social studies program placing into practice the assumptions derived from societal needs and learning theory. Examples of goal statements derived from the previously stated assumptions are as follows:

The social studies component will prepare teachers who will

1. Provide opportunities for students to engage in the process of rational decision making.
2. Actively participate in the multicultural society.
3. Stimulate the moral development of their students.
4. Provide the framework for organization of data through concepts and generalizations from the social sciences and related areas.
5. Use a variety of instructional modes depending on the needs of their students.
6. Guide students through a variety of inquiry processes.
7. Encourage and aid students in examining and clarifying their own values.
8. Model the behaviors expected of their students.

The next step is the specification of teaching competencies and instructional objectives for each of the goal statements. Normally, two or three competencies would flow from each of the statements. Instructional objectives would specify the desired teacher behaviors related to each competency.

Social studies competencies can be grouped into four general components: (1) Goal Determination in the Social Studies; (2) Instructional Design, Strategies, and Materials in the Social Studies; (3) Implementation and Demonstration in Social Studies; and (4) Consequence and Evaluation in the Social Studies. Competency statements and instructional objectives for each component can be illustrated as follows:

Social Studies Methods Component I

Goal Determination in the Social Studies
The student will be able to establish social studies goals for a classroom of students. The student will be able to defend the goals he or she has established in terms of the needs and interests of children and the needs and interests of society, and prove that within the established goals he or she has maintained the integrity of the social sciences.
1. Analyzing and evaluating primary educational purposes as a variable in establishing social studies instructional goals:
    1.1 Given literature reflecting various positions regarding the goals of social studies education, the student will be able to identify at least three philosophical po-

sitions for teaching social studies and explain the relationship of purpose, content, and methodology for each position.
- 1.2 Given a set of social studies instructional goals, the student will be able to identify and describe the primary educational purpose reflected in each goal.
- 1.3 Given various social studies instructional goals, the student will be able to analyze and evaluate these goals in terms of their consequences for learners.
- 1.4 Having established his or her own beliefs concerning the purposes of social studies, the student will be able to construct and evaluate a set of instructional goals which could serve as the basic framework for developing a comprehensive social studies program.
2. Classifying instructional goals into categories of instructional purpose:
    - 2.1 The student will be able to construct social studies instructional goals which reflect the educational purposes of skills development, information acquisition, conceptual development, intellectual process development, interpersonal relations, and intrapersonal relations.
3. Nature of the Social Sciences:
    - 3.1 The student will be able to describe each social science discipline in terms of an imposed body of knowledge, a method of investigation, and a proof process.

Social Studies Methods Component II

Instructional Design, Strategies, and Materials in the Social Studies
The student will be able to design a social studies module using goals determined through the application of knowledges, skills, etc., developed in Component I.
- 1.1 The student will be able to identify the commonalities of social studies instructional design including concepts and generalizations, value orientations, and modes of inquiry.
- 1.2 The student will be able to identify, explain, and demonstrate various models for teaching the social studies.
- 1.3 The student will be able to identify and establish a set of learning materials appropriate to the models used in the learning experiences developed.

Social Studies Methods Component III

Implementation and Demonstration in Social Studies

The student will implement a teaching model or a portion of a model of social studies instruction in an elementary or secondary classroom. During the implementation, the student will demonstrate an understanding of social studies goal determination, instructional design, teaching processes, and student evaluation appropriate to various models of instruction.

Social Studies Methods Component IV

Consequence and Evaluation in the Social Studies

The student will be able to effect an analysis process of what he or she has taught, how he or she has taught it, and the effect of those processes on pupil behavior. The student will use the data gathered to modify his or her social studies goals, designs, and strategies to effect more appropriate behaviors in his or her social studies teaching behaviors.

The four identified components provide a broad range of general competencies that can serve as the starting point for designing the social studies component in a CBTE framework. It must be remembered, however, that in the social studies, more than any other curriculum area, personalization of curriculum and instruction is of the utmost importance. For this reason, the major purpose of the social studies methods component is to provide the student with a range of curriculum and instructional alternatives from which to choose, and to provide practice in making these choices after consideration of at least three major variables—the teacher, the students, and the particular school/community situation in which the student is working.

Experiences in the public schools serve as an integral and important part of the preservice teacher's learning activities. During Phase III of the program, the responsibility of the student in the public school classroom shifts from observer-aide to assuming responsibility for teaching. This is the time that students are able to apply what they have been learning. With the help of the School Based Teacher Educator and the University instructor, the student develops and teaches lessons involving concept attainment exercises, concept development through simulation and gaming techniques, teaching and integrating map and globe skills in the overall program, etc. This is a time when students can apply inquiry skills in teaching a social studies lesson and chart the progress of their pupils over an extended period of time. At the same time that the student is demonstrating social studies competencies, he is required to continuously demonstrate proficiency in the competencies developed in the two preceding phases. The social studies component is not an isolated experience, as was so often the case in traditional methods courses.

Testing the Model for Exit and Recycling

The final phase of the CBTE model places the student in a school setting for an extended teaching experience. It is at this point that the student is held responsible for integrating previous learning experiences into a meaningful, full-time teaching/learning situation. The student is encouraged to develop his or her own teaching style and at the same time to analyze the results of teaching behaviors in relation to the stated objectives and consequences. During this phase, the student is expected to draw upon every conceivable bit of knowledge and skill to orchestrate a healthy and positive teaching-learning situation.

This exit phase assumes added importance in that it becomes the testing ground for the social studies component and the CBTE program. The success or failure of the student teacher is used as one measure of the effectiveness of the preservice training program. The student teacher is assisted in competency demonstration through a program of clinical supervision in the field. Trained supervisory personnel work with individual students to help them analyze and assess their teaching and to identify specific programs of instruction which might be needed to assist preservice teachers in meeting program standards.

Evaluation of social studies teaching and learning is correlated with the stated objectives and agreed upon competencies. Even though competency demonstration is assessed during the social studies component, students are expected to demonstrate certain social studies competencies during student teaching. To illustrate, the following are examples of assessment guidelines used to evaluate student teaching in social studies:

- Justifies objectives and plans in terms of recognized curriculum guidelines and the characteristics of a particular teaching situation.

- Selects and uses a variety of films, books, current publications, documents, etc., to support learning objectives.
- Identifies and selects materials and resources compatible with objectives for a given pupil population.
- Organizes knowledge acquisition strategies around concepts and generalizations.
- Plans for valuing strategies that allow students to form and/or clarify their own values.
- Designs strategies to teach the use of scientific modes of inquiry and techniques of social scientists as tools for solving problems, making decisions, or applying and processing knowledge.
- Develops strategies to encourage pupil participation in social action projects.
- Identifies positive and negative attributes in teaching toward concept attainment.
- Uses dilemmas and questioning strategies to identify and clarify values.
- Uses questioning techniques consistent with a values clarification model.
- Helps students recognize the role of values in human behavior.
- Involves pupils in both independent and group inquiry.
- Involves pupils in situations which require the application of critical thinking skills to identify problem solutions and/or make decisions.
- Selects and implements activities to develop skills in gathering, processing, and analyzing data.
- Assists pupils in planning and implementing a social action project based on identified social studies goals and objectives.
- Identifies and implements activities for social participation through simulation, gaming, and role-playing.[4]

Primary emphasis is to obtain data for feedback to students. Such information is used as a point of departure for discussion purposes. The School Based Teacher Educator, college instructor, and student teacher specify and agree upon the competencies to be demonstrated prior to teaching and observation. The purpose always is to focus on the consequences of a teaching act as it relates to assumptions, goals, and objectives and to use analysis of teaching behaviors as a means of professional improvement.

Integrating the social studies component in a CBTE model is more than redesigning content into a different format. Too many programs have failed through this approach. It is not enough merely to "competency base" a traditional social studies methods course. To successfully integrate this component within an instructional system, the "gestalt" of the total process must be considered. The student must be able to understand and relate component parts of the program in order to move with confidence and success through the preservice experience. Social studies must become an interlocking part in a chain of experiences designed to produce a competent teacher.

Footnotes

[1] For a detailed description of the University of Houston program, see B. Dell Felder and Wilford A. Weber, "Competency Based Teacher Education: The University of Houston Experience," *Texas Tech Journal of Education* (Winter, 1975), pp. 147–161.

[2] "Attachment Three: The Professional Preparation Program," Bench Mark Data on the Undergraduate Professional Teacher Preparation Program, Unpublished Memorandum from Loye Y. Hollis, College of Education, University of Houston, March 1, 1976, pp. 9–10.

[3] Developed in cooperation with Don Baden, University of Illinois at Edwardsville.

[4] Adapted from materials developed by Sarah White, University of Houston.

Part Three

Issues and Opportunities

At an earlier point in our history, there was greater clarity about what social values were desirable and how responsibilities for helping children develop them would be shared among the home, school, and community. Today such clarity is replaced by confusion and conflict over which values should be emphasized. There is concern that the overall development of children and youth is seriously threatened by the absence of experiences which foster the development of character and citizenship. Social studies teachers find themselves in the middle of this dilemma, for it is clear that the social studies is expected to assume a major responsibility in this area.

Some argue that CBTE programs do not prepare teachers to work effectively in the affective areas. They contend that such programs teach only those things which can be measured and thus ignore those teaching behaviors associated with affective development; for, more often than not, such behaviors defy precise description, let alone exact measurement.

In Chapters 5 and 6 Wilford A. Weber, Jane McCarthy Goldstein, and Geneva Gay challenge such criticisms. Weber and Goldstein assert that CBTE programs will reflect the assumptions and values of those who design and implement them. Those CBTE program designers who are concerned about the affective development of children will also be concerned about preparing teachers to work effectively in these areas.

Gay examines CBTE in relation to multicultural education. Social studies has only recently defined its position with respect to the outcomes of multicultural education for children. Her suggestions regarding the competencies that teachers will need to be effective in helping children develop skills needed for living in a culturally pluralistic society provide new insights for the preparation of social studies teachers.

There is nothing in the philosophy or practice of CBTE which says that only those things which can be accurately measured are worthy of inclusion in the preparation programs of teachers. Indeed, the opposite would more likely be argued: that those things considered important to the development of effective teaching behaviors should be included in preparation programs, and efforts should be intensified to develop more effective means for measurement and assessment.

In Chapter 7, Thomas W. Hewitt probes beyond the preservice preparation of teachers into the realm of continuing professional development. He points out that opportunities for teachers to update their professional knowledge and skills are presently very limited. Teaching will not attain full professional status until there is opportunity for all teachers to update themselves continuously to new findings in the professional culture. Such opportunities must be reality based; they must meet the needs of both schools as institutions and teachers as individual professionals. CBTE, if applied to meeting the inservice and continuing professional development needs of teachers, could provide the means to achieve this end.

5 Affective Teaching Competencies and Competency Based Teacher Education

Wilford A. Weber and Jane McCarthy Goldstein

Introduction

There are those who view competency based education as the antithesis of affective education. They claim that the very nature of competency based education makes it impossible for competency based teacher education programs to address the needs of affective education. They insist that competency based teacher education programs are necessarily mechanistic, dehumanizing, and depersonalizing. Such assertions are without merit.

The purpose of this chapter is to make a case for the position that competency based teacher education programs can be—and should be—designed to address the needs of affective education. It is argued that properly designed competency based teacher education programs have the capacity to prepare teachers who have the ability and the desire to use affective education approaches effectively with their students.

Teacher education program design may be thought of as consisting of two major tasks. The first of these is the process of establishing the objectives of the instructional program. More specifically, this process consists of identifying and specifying the knowledge, skills, and attitudes—the competencies—thought to be needed by teachers. It is argued here that this first task—the specification of teacher competencies—is best accomplished when competencies are derived from a carefully conceptualized teacher role model. That is, the view held here is that competency statements should describe those understandings, behaviors, and attitudes that program designers believe a teacher must be able to demonstrate in order to facilitate the achievement of those student outcomes deemed desirable. Thus, the specification of teacher competencies builds on the specification of desired student outcomes.

The second task consists of determining and describing the most effective and efficient means for achieving the objectives of the instructional program. This process consists of specifying the operational characteristics of an instructional system which is intended to help teacher education students acquire and demonstrate those teacher competencies specified as instructional program objectives. It is argued here that a competency based instructional system is particularly well suited for this purpose. The position taken here is that competency based instructional systems have the precision necessary to help students become competent professionals and the flexibility necessary to preserve the individuality of those students.

Although the discussion thus far has dealt with the two major teacher education program design tasks—the specification of teacher competencies and the specification of instructional system characteristics—in very general terms, the purpose of this chapter is to examine these tasks in relation to the social studies and affective education. That is, the intent here is to discuss a very limited aspect of the teacher education program design process. First, the discussion is limited to the professional education of social studies teachers. Second, within that context, the focus is on affective education. Specifically, this chapter examines three assumptions in this regard:

1. The social studies place heavy emphasis on the use of affective education approaches to develop affective as well as cognitive student outcomes.
2. The social studies teacher needs certain teaching competencies—understandings, skills, and attitudes—if he or she is to use affective education approaches effectively to foster the achievement of desired student outcomes.
3. A competency based instructional system can help teacher education students acquire and demonstrate those teaching competencies needed if they are to use affective education approaches effectively.

Student Outcomes

Although the events of the past decade make a *prima facie* case in support of the assumption that the social studies place heavy emphasis on the use of affective education approaches to develop affective as well as cognitive student outcomes, it is clear that the social studies have long stressed the importance of affective student learning. It can be argued that social studies teachers have always been involved in affective education. Instruction in good citizenship, patriotism, and democratic values was one of the earliest approaches. Effort was made to promote sound, moral character development. Early social studies teachers were also expected to serve as role models for their students. They were to be examples of the virtues of patriotism, punctuality, honesty, and personal responsibility.

However, as Hunt and Metcalf note, the early attempts at affective education relied on a system of rewards and punishments. Good behavior was rewarded and bad behavior was punished. These attempts led to hypocrisy and cynicism on the part of both teachers and students. Students were being indoctrinated in values to which most adults paid only lip service. There was no attempt to provide students with a method of examining societal or personal values. They were not given the tools necessary to make rational choices between alternative values.[1]

The 1960s brought the emergence of a number of new models of affective education in the social studies. These approaches included value clarification, value analysis, the examination of controversial issues, humanistic education, and moral development.[2] For example, in 1967, Fenton called for the inclusion of affective education in the social studies curriculum. He suggested that students be challenged to examine their own values and the consequences of holding those values. Fenton also suggested that students examine alternative values and their consequences and learn to provide evidence to support their beliefs. He considered citizenship training to be a combination of attitudes and values, inquiry skills, and knowledge of content.[3]

During that same year, Hunt and Metcalf provided a model of value analysis which included concept analysis and a consideration of consequences. The goal of value analysis, according to their model, was to produce students who were consistent in their values and able to justify their values by using criteria developed from a philosophy of life. Hunt and Metcalf considered the development of this philosophy to be one of the most important decisions the students would make in their lives. They argued that the only justification for instruction in social studies was to facilitate the reflective testing of beliefs.[4]

A year earlier, Raths, Harmin, and Simon published their model for value clarification. The approach consisted of seven steps which included making choices, examining the consequences of those choices, and acting upon those choices. The value clarification approach has generated a wealth of curriculum materials and activities as social studies educators responded to the approach with enthusiasm.[5]

The 1960s also saw the emergence of moral education and, in particular, Lawrence Kohlberg's very popular cognitive-developmental approach to moral education. Kohlberg's theory states that an individual's reasoning about moral issues progresses through six identifiable stages. These stages are moved through in sequence, although some people may spend less time in one stage than in others. Stages progress from lower-order reasoning to higher-order reasoning.[6]

The past ten years have seen an increasing commitment to affective education, value analysis, value clarification, moral education, and other variations on this general theme. It is clear that social studies educators favor various affective education approaches and value the types of student outcomes which result from the use of those approaches. Evidence of this can be found elsewhere in this publication. Jarolimek's chapter on the basics in social studies presents six "basics" which appear to reflect a concern for the types of learner outcomes affective education is intended to produce.

In summary, then, with regard to the first assumption examined here, it may be said that there is ample and growing evidence that the social studies do place heavy emphasis on the use of a variety of affective education approaches with the intent to develop affective as well as cognitive student learning. Indeed, the evidence suggests that affective education which emphasizes the development of affective learner outcomes may be the *sine qua non* of the social studies.

Affective Teaching Competencies

Having established the importance of affective education in the social studies curriculum, the next task is to examine questions related to the specification of teaching competencies supportive of affective education. As noted earlier, the assumption here is that the social studies teacher needs certain understandings, skills, and attitudes if he or she is to use affective education approaches effectively to facilitate the achievement of desired student outcomes.

Those who describe the process of teacher education generally agree that teachers need to possess and display certain understandings and skills if they are to be effective. This position is perhaps best expressed in *Educating a Profession*, the

Report of the Bicentennial Commission on Education for the Profession of Teaching of the American Association of Colleges for Teacher Education. The report asserts that "a professional teacher is one who possesses a broad repertoire of classroom behaviors and skills, grounded in professional and academic knowledge."[7] In addition, there is overwhelming support for the position that teacher education programs ought to help teachers acquire those understandings and skills deemed desirable.

Literature which discusses the teacher's role relevant to affective education in the social studies supports these positions. For example, Beyer, in describing the teacher's use of Kohlberg's moral dilemmas in the classroom, specifies some of the teacher knowledge and skills needed to lead moral discussions.[8] Among these are: the ability to ask students nonthreatening questions; the ability to establish and maintain a supportive classroom atmosphere; the ability to encourage and sustain student-to-student interaction; the ability to identify and cope with diversions; and the ability to locate and prepare moral dilemmas and to write and employ lesson plans for their use. Others who have advocated affective education have presented similar listings.

What is perhaps the most comprehensive listing of social studies teacher competencies is contained in a report of The Task Force to Study Programs Leading to Certification for Teachers of Social Studies. The task force described social studies teachers' competencies in the affective area, the cognitive area, and the community, school, and professional relations areas. The task force first specified student social studies outcomes deemed desirable. It next identified those teacher behaviors likely to facilitate the achievement of those student outcomes. And finally, the task force described those teacher competencies which were thought to facilitate the teacher behaviors identified. This process resulted in a sixty-page listing of social studies teacher competencies. About half of those competencies—over three hundred and fifty—are concerned with the affective area.[9]

In short, then, there is a great deal of support for the position that teachers need certain understandings and skills—knowledge and performance teaching competencies—in order to implement affective education successfully. Additionally, there is growing support for the notion that teachers also need certain attitudes—affective teaching competencies—in order to be maximally effective. For example, the report of the Bicentennial Commission suggests that "not only must preparation programs develop teaching skills and a knowledge of theoretical and empirical concepts, but they must foster humanistic educational values and attitudes."[10] As might be expected, this viewpoint is widely supported by advocates of affective education. For example, Sweeney and Parsons discuss several attitudes they believe crucial to the effective use of affective education approaches. These include: the teacher's willingness to have his or her own values tested; the teacher's willingness to engage in self-reflection; the teacher's willingness to share leadership with students; and the teacher's willingness to utilize new teaching techniques and to allow students to participate in the selection of curriculum content.[11]

Because there is overwhelming support for the position that teachers—and social studies teachers in particular—need certain affective teaching competencies if they are to use effectively affective education, it would be expected that teacher education programs would be designed to foster such competencies. Unfortunately, this is not the case. Few teacher education programs intentionally develop affective teacher competencies. The reasons for this are many.

Problems concerning the specification of affective teaching competencies stem from an important question: Is it possible and desirable to specify affective teaching competencies as teacher education program outcomes; that is, can and should affective teaching competencies be specified as program requirements the teacher education student is expected to acquire and demonstrate?

The very nature of this question requires an answer which is far more opinion than fact. That is, teacher educators who address this question in the process of conceptualizing and designing a teacher education program make program design decisions which are a blend of their professional judgments and personal preferences—decisions which are a mixture of beliefs about what can be done and attitudes about what should be done. Most program design decisions—including those decisions having to do with the specification of affective teaching competencies—are necessarily program specific. In each program, decisions regarding teaching affective competencies reflect the beliefs and attitudes of the teacher educators who have conceptualized and designed that program. Thus, great differences of opinion exist. The discussion which follows briefly describes and analyzes the beliefs and values which account for some of these differences.

The question asks: Can and should affective teacher competencies be specified as program expectations? The position that a particular teacher education program designer takes in responding to this question is dependent on his or her assumptions. The following are viewed as the most common of these; they are presented as conditional statements:

1. If a program designer operationally defines competencies as those particular teacher understandings, behaviors, and attitudes thought to facilitate the achievement of desirable learner outcomes, it is likely that he or she would favor the specification and inclusion of affective competencies. On the other hand, if a program designer defines competencies as teaching skills only, he or she is not at all likely to support the specification of affective competencies.
2. If a program designer believes that competencies should be generated from a well-conceptualized model of the teacher's role—a conceptualization of what that role is, what it ought to be, and what it may become—and if his or her role model conceives the effective teacher as one who manifests particular attitudes and values, then it is highly probable that he or she would feel a need to specify affective competencies which deal with those identified attitudes and values. However, if a program designer's role model does not attend to the issue of teacher attitude and values, it is not likely that he or she would see a need to specify affective competencies.
3. If a program designer believes that competencies must be described in a manner which adequately communicates the program's expectations of the student and if he or she also believes that affective competencies can be described in terms which are sufficiently explicit to serve the function of communicating program expectations, it is very likely that he or she would specify affective competencies. But if a designer feels that affective competencies do not lend themselves to the level of explicitness required, it is very unlikely that he or she would attempt to include affective competencies.
4. If a program designer takes the position that competencies should be specified on the basis of their perceived importance regardless of questions concerning the precision and ease with which those competencies might be measured and assessed, he or she is more likely to specify affective competencies than if he or she feels that measurement concerns should influence the selection of the competencies to be included. Indeed, a program designer who feels that competencies must be measured and assessed with great precision and who feels that the many measurement and assessment problems associated with affective behaviors preclude

adequate measurement would not specify affective competencies.
5. If a program designer feels that competencies should be specified and included when there is good and sufficient reason to believe that the competencies are related to teaching effectiveness, and if he or she feels that such relationships exist with regard to certain affective teacher behaviors, it is probable that he or she would specify and include affective competencies. However, if a program designer feels that competencies should be specified and included only if empirically validated relationships have been established between those competencies and desirable learner outcomes, it is likely that he or she would specify and include few, if any, affective competencies.
6. If a program designer believes that teacher education student attitudes and values can and should be influenced and shaped by the program, he or she is far more likely to specify affective competencies as program expectations than if he or she believes that student attitudes and values cannot or should not be influenced.[12]

In summary, then, it is argued here that the designers of teacher education programs are most likely to specify affective competencies when they believe that: (1) the term competency should be defined to include teacher attitudes; (2) the effective teacher is one who exhibits particular attitudes and values; (3) affective competencies can be described in terms which are sufficiently explicit; (4) competencies should be specified on the basis of their perceived importance without regard for measurement concerns; (5) there are good and sufficient reasons to suggest that certain affective teacher behaviors are related to desirable learner outcomes; and (6) teacher education student attitudes can and should be influenced and shaped by instruction. Program designers who hold differing beliefs are not likely to specify affective competencies in the course of designing their programs. The position here is that they should. Indeed, they must if they would train social studies teachers to use affective education approaches.

Instructional System Characteristics

Even if the decision is made to specify affective teaching competencies—and knowledge and performance competencies—for inclusion in a teacher education program's de-

PROFESSIONALIZING SOCIAL STUDIES TEACHING

sign and even if those competencies are identified and specified, program designers face one last major design task: the specification of the operational characteristics of the instructional system which is intended to help teachers acquire and demonstrate those competencies.

Earlier in this chapter, it was asserted that competency based instructional systems have the potential to help teacher education students develop knowledge, performance, and affective competencies because they offer precision and flexibility. It is argued here that competency based instructional systems are particularly well suited to facilitate the acquisition and demonstration of affective teaching competencies. Again, the key notions are those of precision and flexibility.[13]

Thorough descriptions of competency based instruction are available in the literature[14] and elsewhere in this publication. No attempt will be made to present such descriptions here. However, it does seem sensible to focus on what are considered here to be the two major advantages of competency based instructional systems relevant to the professional education of social studies teachers: precision and flexibility.

Competency based teacher education programs have been described as instructional systems in which: (1) the competencies to be demonstrated by the teacher education student are specified and made public; (2) the criteria and procedures to be used in assessing the competency of the student are made explicit and public; and (3) the student is held accountable for the demonstration—not the acquisition—of those competencies.[15] It is these three notions which distinguish competency based instruction from more traditional approaches and which provide both precision and flexibility.

Precision is enhanced by the principle that the expected outcomes of the program—the competencies the student is expected to demonstrate—are made explicit and public. It is in this way that the purposes of the system become clearly articulated and understood; it is in this way that the system becomes purposive. Program design efforts take those purposes into account. Consequently, the various components of the instructional system are more likely to be consistent with the program's goals and contribute to their achievement if those purposes are clearly specified, communicated, and understood. It is argued that this greater precision in specifying the purpose of the instructional system increases the potential for program effectiveness and efficiency while encouraging the inclusion of affective teaching competencies as program expectations.

Logic suggests that if the competencies needed by teachers are identified and specified and if—as suggested by Elam in his discussion of the essential elements of a competency based teacher education program—"the instructional program is intended to facilitate the development and evaluation of the student's achievement of competencies specified,"[16] the likelihood of developing those competencies is enhanced. In short, a purposive system is more likely to achieve its goals than a program which is not purposive or which has ill-defined goals.

Flexibility, on the other hand, is enhanced by the principle that the teacher education student is held accountable for the demonstration—not the acquisition—of the specified competencies. This principle increases the possibility that the instructional system is individualized and personalized.

Hall and Jones have said that a competency based education program "cannot be successful without some form of personalization.... Personalization means individualization of instruction that includes responses to the personal feelings and psychosocial growth needs of the learner as well."[17]

In describing competency based teacher education programs, Weber and Rathbone have asserted that: (1) a given instructional objective or activity must be appropriate to the interests, abilities, and learning styles of the student, and (2) procedures for diagnosing individual needs must be designed to permit the student to develop a realistic self-awareness so that he or she can design his or her personal program.[18] They add that competency based education programs provide for self-paced instruction, alternative routes of instruction, and student involvement in the design of his or her instructional experiences. In short, competency based instructional systems may be designed to provide the kind of psychological environment most likely to facilitate the development of those affective competencies needed by the social studies teacher.

Once again turning to *Educating a Profession*, one finds a statement which points up the advantages of the precision and flexibility provided by competency based instructional systems.

> CBTE is a technical means meant to achieve a major end—the development of highly knowledgeable, socially committed, multiskilled, and humanistic professionals.... Competency based training processes must themselves exemplify the best qualities and practices of the humanistic professionals they mean to produce.[19]

Summary

Because the social studies place such heavy emphasis on the use of affective education approaches, it has been suggested here that it is necessary that social studies teachers develop those teaching competencies needed for the effective use of those approaches. It has been argued that certain of those needed teaching competencies are affective competencies and those which are identified should be specified as program expectations. Further, it has been suggested that teacher education programs can be and should be designed in ways which indicate a clear intent to facilitate the teacher education student's development of those affective teaching competencies which are identified as needed. Finally, it has been claimed that competency based instructional systems provide a precision and a flexibility which enhance the potential for the successful development of affective teaching competencies.

The assumptions on which these arguments are based appear to be logically sound. However, it remains for these assumptions to be tested by the rigors of practice. It is hoped that they will be.

Footnotes

[1] Maurice P. Hunt and Lawrence E. Metcalf, *Teaching High School Social Studies* (New York: Harper and Row Publishers, 1968).

[2] Jean Fair, ed., *National Assessment and Social Studies Education. A Review of Assessments in Citizenship and Social Studies by the National Council for the Social Studies* (Washington, D.C.: National Council for the Social Studies, 1975).

[3] Edwin Fenton, *The New Social Studies* (New York: Holt, Rinehart, and Winston, Inc., 1967).

[4] Maurice P. Hunt and Lawrence E. Metcalf, *Teaching High School Social Studies*.

[5] Louis E. Raths, Merrill Harmin and Sidney B. Simon, *Values and Teaching* (Columbus, Ohio: Charles E. Merrill Publishing Co., 1966).

[6] Lawrence Kohlberg, *Stages in the Development of Moral Thought and Action* (New York: Holt, Rinehart, and Winston, Inc., 1970).

[7] Robert B. Howsam and others, *Educating a Profession*, A Report of the Bicentennial Commission on Education for the Profession of Teaching of the American Association of Colleges for Teacher Education (Washington, D.C.: American Association of Colleges for Teacher Education, 1976), p. 88.

[8] Barry K. Beyer, "Conducting Moral Discussions in the Classroom," *Social Education*, Vol. 40, No. 4 (April 1976), pp. 194–202.

[9] Minnesota Department of Education, *Social Studies Teacher Competencies*, Papers developed by The Task Force to Study Programs Leading to Certification for Teachers of Social Studies reprinted by the Multi-State Consortium on Performance-Based Teacher Education (Albany, New York: The State Education Department, 1973).

[10] Robert B. Howsam and others, *Educating a Profession*, p. 89.

[11] Jo A. Cutler Sweeney and James B. Parsons, "Teacher Preparation and Models for Teaching Controversial Social Issues," *Controversial Issues in the Social Studies: A Contemporary Perspective*, Raymond H. Muessig, ed. (Washington, D.C.: National Council for the Social Studies, 1975), pp. 45–83.

[12] Wilford A. Weber, "Competency Based Teacher Education: The Specification and Assessment of Affective Competencies." Paper presented at the annual meeting of the American Educational Research Association (San Francisco, April 1976).

[13] Robert B. Howsam, "Competency Based Instruction." A paper presented at a meeting of the Classroom Teachers Association (Washington, D.C., November 1971).

[14] James M. Cooper, Howard L. Jones, and Wilford A. Weber, "Specifying Teacher Competencies," *Journal of Teacher Education*, Vol. 24, No. 1 (Spring 1973), pp. 17–33; James M. Cooper, Wilford A. Weber, and Charles E. Johnson, eds., *Competency Based Teacher Education: A Systems Approach to Program Design* (Berkeley, California; McCutchan Publishing Corporation, 1973); Stanley Elam, *Performance-Based Teacher Education*, PBTE Series: No. 1. (Washington, D.C.: American Association of Colleges for Teacher Education, 1971); Gene E. Hall and Howard L. Jones, *Competency-Based Education: A Process for the Improvement of Education* (Englewood Cliffs, New Jersey: Prentice-Hall, Inc., 1976); W. Robert Houston, ed., *Exploring Competency Based Education* (Berkeley, California: McCutchan Publishing Corporation, 1974); W. Robert Houston and Robert B. Howsam, eds., *Competency-Based Teacher Education: Progress, Problems, and Prospects* (Chicago: Science Research Associates, Inc., 1972); Wilford A. Weber, "Designing and Operating a Competency-Based Program in Teacher Education," *Competency Based Education: Theory, Practice, and Evaluation*, Paul M. Halverson, ed. (Athens: University of Georgia, 1975), pp. 39–57; Wilford A. Weber, James J. Cooper, and W. Robert Houston. *A Guide to Competency Based Teacher Education* (Westfield, Texas: Competency Based Instructional Systems, 1973); and Wilford A. Weber, "Program Conceptualization and Design," *Programmatic Issues in Teacher Education*, Ruben Dario Olivarez, ed. (Austin: The University of Texas, 1975), pp. 1–11.

[15] James M. Cooper, Wilford A. Weber, and Charles E. Johnson, eds., *Compentency Based Teacher Education: A Systems Approach to Program Design*.

[16] Stanley Elam, *Performance-Based Teacher Education*, PBTE Series: No. 1, p. 7.

[17] Gene E. Hall and Howard L. Jones, *Competency-Based Education: A Process for the Improvement of Education*, p. 13.

[18] Wilford A. Weber and Charles Rathbone, "Developing Instructional Strategies," *Competency Based Teacher Education: A Systems Approach to Program Design*, James M. Cooper, Wilford A. Weber, and Charles E. Johnson, eds., p. 60.

[19] Robert B. Howsam and others, *Educating a Profession*, pp. 134–135.

6 Interfacing CBTE and Multicultural Education in Social Studies Teacher Preparation

Geneva Gay

The Questions: Who Is Asking What?

What is "basic" or essential in the preparation of social studies teachers and in social studies instruction for students? How is the issue of multicultural education related to these? The current emphasis in the educational arena on "basics" and the harsh realities of limited funding and declining enrollments are having their toll on social studies and multicultural education programs alike. Social studies programs are being cut to a bare minimum and, in many instances, separate multicultural education programs are being eliminated entirely. However, the program sacrifices forced by strident economic conditions are not necessarily a reflection of the importance of the need for multicultural education and the role of social studies teachers in its implementation.

Demands for multicultural education in some form continue to persist, as evidenced, for example, by the persistence of its advocates and different ethnic groups, by its inclusion in lists of competencies for high school graduation, and by ethnic heritage federal and state legislation. College professors, school administrators, and curriculum leaders are asking more questions about what constitutes multicultural teacher preparation in general and in the context of particular subjects or areas of specialization, such as early childhood education, science education, and social studies education. Assumptions that teachers who are effective with any students can teach all kinds of students and that teachers need no special training in how to teach multicultural education increasingly are subject to skepticism. Questions are being asked about the plausibility of interfacing the concepts of competency based (CBTE) and multicultural education (MCE) in the preparation programs of social studies teachers.

In this age of competencies and accountability, nebulous and ambiguous descriptions that social studies teachers are being responsive to ethnic differences and multiculturalism if they respect students from different ethnic backgrounds and include information about ethnic groups' contributions in their curriculum content are inadequate and will no longer suffice. The question is what constitutes respectfulness and responsiveness in reference to teachers' knowledge and instructional behaviors in implementing multicultural curricula and interacting with ethnically and culturally different students. Teacher training programs must be much more concrete and specific in outlining expectations, objectives, and behavioral consequences of teacher education students relative to multicultural knowledge and skills. In effect, they must ask, and attempt to answer, the question: What must social studies teachers know and be able to do in order to teach multicultural education effectively within the parameters of the social studies? The potential exists for a viable connection to be made between the concepts of CBTE and multicultural social studies teacher education. It is possible because of the quest for more specificity, coherency, organization, and sequential development in designing multicultural programs for training social studies teachers.

Potential Relationship Between CBTE, Social Studies, and MCE

Hersh describes performance or competency based teacher education as a *process* for program planning in teacher education, not a specific *program* of teacher preparation.[1] This process uses a systems approach to identifying teacher needs, sequencing objectives and learning experiences, accommodating individual differences, and determining if needs have been met or objectives have been achieved. According to Cooper, Jones, and Weber, CBTE programs are composed of three major kinds of competencies. These are: (1) knowledge competencies which specify cognitive understandings, (2) performance competencies which specify teaching or instructional behaviors and attitudes, and (3) consequence competencies which identify student behaviors that are to result from teacher behaviors and are indicators of teacher effectiveness.[2] Houston describes two additional categories of competencies. These are affective competencies which identify teacher attitudes to be demonstrated, and exploratory or expressive competencies which specify experiences to be undertaken by teacher education students.[3] Most advocates of CBTE agree that the most desirable point of departure for identifying competencies is to begin by specifying the kinds of emotional, intellectual, social, and physical growth teachers hope to achieve in students. Once these are determined, it becomes easier for one to identify the knowledge and performance competencies that will facilitate the desired student outcomes.

Translated to the domain of social studies teacher education, the fundamental questions to be addressed in planning and implementing competency based programs are: What should teachers *know* to be effective in teaching social studies to students? What should teachers be able to *do* to be effective in teaching social studies to students? How should student behaviors change as a direct consequence of teachers' performance, or what *influences* should social studies teachers have on students' behavior? In competency based programs, emphases shift from knowledge acquisition of the social studies curriculum projects and instructional techniques, which predominate in conventional social studies teacher preparation programs, to *demonstrated* performance mastery of knowledge and instructional methodologies and the *impact* of instruction on student learning and growth.

Examples of knowledge competencies for social studies teachers inherent in the first question might include the ability to identify Bloom's taxonomy in questioning strategies; to describe the major steps in the inquiry mode of teaching; to understand the taxonomy of affective objectives in the context of social studies content and goals; to distinguish between inductive and deductive reasoning; to define a fact, concept, generalization, and theory; to characterize the different stages of cognitive moral reasoning; and to distinguish among the scientific modes of inquiry used by different social science disciplines. Performance competencies might include the ability to ask and distinguish questions at all levels of Bloom's taxonomy; to use values clarification techniques; to use inquiry teaching strategies; to recognize stage 2 from stage 3 reasoning in moral dilemma discussions; and to write concepts, theories, and generalizations. Sample outcomes social studies teachers might expect to bring about in the social, emotional, and intellectual growth of their students—consequence competencies—include improving students' abilities to distinguish facts from opinions; increasing the frequency of students' use of high order responses (on the taxonomy levels of analysis, synthesis, and evaluation) in class discussions; getting students to use the skills of data collection and information processing in problem-solving and decision-making; increasing students' participation in group consensus activities; and succeeding in getting students who initially fluctuated between stage 2 and stage 3 reasoning in moral dilemmas to reason consistently at stage 3.

In general the formative questions in designing competency based *multicultural* education programs for social studies teachers are the same as for any competency based program. Differences occur in the content and contextual frames of reference in which the competencies are to be demonstrated. The teacher competencies to be achieved dictate the questions to be asked, and the areas of emphasis determine the content specifications of the program. The first question to be asked in multicultural competency based social studies teacher preparation deals with cognitive competencies. It asks: What do social studies teachers need to *know* about the content of ethnic diversity and cultural pluralism in American history, life, and culture to teach social studies from multicultural and multiethnic perspectives? An equally important companion question is: What do social studies teachers need to know about ethnic groups' cultures, life styles, values, heritages, and learning styles to teach social studies effectively to ethnically different students? The specification of performance competencies results from responses to the question: What is it that social studies teachers need to be able to *do* to be effective in teaching multicultural education in the social studies content areas, and in teaching social studies to culturally different students? The third category of competencies has to do with the outcomes of teachers' instructional behaviors in teaching multiculturalism in the social studies, as evidenced by changes in students' behaviors. The instructive question is: What *influences* should social studies teachers have on students' knowledge, attitudes, and behaviors relative to ethnic pluralism and cultural diversity?

Unquestionably, social studies teachers have a responsibility to become involved actively in the implementation of multicultural education. Their content areas are perceived by many as the most natural vehicles of the total school curricula through which students can be exposed to multicultural education. CBTE is a potentially viable strategy for designing programs to prepare social studies teachers to teach multicultural education, and it deserves more careful consideration. It provides a mechanism for designers of teacher education programs to operationalize their commitment to multicultural education; to include a greater degree of specificity in the focus, content, and experiences in multiculturalism made available to teachers in training; to better assess and evaluate teacher achievement in multicultural education; and to hold teachers accountable for mastery of basic competencies in multicultural education as an essential aspect of their overall professional preparation.

Interfacing MCE and CBTE in Teacher Preparation: Previous Explorations and Sample Antecedents

Banks and Gay have made some observations about ethnic studies and multicultural education programs designed for students that are generalizable to an even greater degree to multicultural preparation programs for teachers. Banks notes that few of the attempts to implement ethnic studies programs "are sound because their goals remain confused, ambiguous, and conflicting. Many ... have been structured without careful planning and clear rationales," and "divergent goals of ethnic studies programs are often voiced by experts of many different persuasions and ideologies."[4] Gay advises that "the potential of education to help students develop understanding of and acceptance for the validity of cultural pluralism and ethnic diversity in American life will not be realized unless some well-defined systematic approaches are employed to revise school curricula so that they will be pluralistic."[5] The competency based model has the potential for diminishing these problems by bringing more structure, focus, and internal consistency to the process of planning multicultural teacher education programs.

In 1976 the National Council for the Social Studies published *Curriculum Guidelines for Multiethnic Education*. This document sets some parameters for multicultural social studies teacher education. It recommends that preservice and inservice programs help teachers:

(a) clarify and analyze their feelings, attitudes, and perceptions toward their own and other ethnic groups; (b) acquire content about and understanding of the historical experiences and sociological characteristics of American ethnic groups; (c) increase their instructional skills within multiethnic school environments; (d) improve their skill in curriculum development as it relates to ethnic pluralism; and (e) increase their skill in creating, selecting, evaluating, and revising instructional materials.[6]

Baker, Banks, and Aragon each has developed somewhat different models for multicultural teacher education. Although similar, these models were developed independently of each other and of the NCSS *Curriculum Guidelines for Multiethnic Education*. According to Baker, the three critical components of multicultural education for teachers are acquisition of knowledge, development of a philosophy of education consistent with the goals of cultural pluralism, and involvement in the implementation of multicultural content.[7] Banks talks about preparation programs helping teachers acquire attitudes, conceptual frameworks, knowledge, and skills to facilitate the implementation of multiethnic education.[8] Like Baker, Aragon's model for multicultural teacher education includes three components: awareness or cognitive understanding of ethnic diversity; application of awareness in analyzing programs, teaching styles, learning theories, and instructional resources and materials; and the logistics of implementation.[9] None of the components of these multicultural teacher education models is an exact parallel to the three kinds of competencies of CBTE. However, conceptually, there are some similarities. Baker's "acquisition" and Aragon's "awareness" components are analogous to knowledge competencies in the CBTE model; Aragon's "application of awareness" and "logistics of implementation," Banks' "skills," and Baker's "involvement" are, in effect, performance competencies; and Baker's "development of a philosophy" and Banks' "conceptual frameworks" are suggestive of consequence competencies.

While Johnson's recommendations for developing multicultural education programs are not organized in a step-phase model as are Baker's and Aragon's, they cover similar areas of importance. She feels:

> It is essential that our schools be staffed with educators who have some sense of self-awareness and understanding of their personal feelings, attitudes, and needs and how these factors affect their interaction with others ... [are] prepared to analyze their behavior in the school environment in order to prevent harmful actions toward youngsters which might derive from the educator's biases, fears, needs, desires, and prejudices ... [are] capable of identifying culturally-related behaviors, strengths, and problems encountered in the school environment ... [can use] that capability ... to plan teaching-learning activities that address the needs of young people relative to all appropriate educational domains ... [are] prepared to accept the basic humanity of all children with all that such acceptance implies ... [are] prepared to teach in such a way that all children ... can be helped to develop to their highest potential.[10]

Similarly, Gay recommends teacher education programs that incorporate activities and experiences designed to help teachers (1) better understand themselves, their racial behaviors, attitudes, and values; (2) learn skills to help students clarify their racial attitudes and values; (3) apply the tools and techniques of social psychology, group dynamics, and ethnography of communications to analyzing classroom dynamics in desegregated settings; and (4) become familiar with the cultural experiences of ethnically different students, including their cultural perspectives, values, customs and mores, communication habits, and interactional styles, and their educational implications.[11]

To date, only a few tentative attempts have been made to interface CBTE with multicultural education.[12] Most of the competencies resulting from these efforts tend to be formative and rather general. Nor are they specified according to particular subject areas. Undoubtedly, this is a reflection, in part, of the relative newness of the concept of multicultural education, and the conflicting conceptions of its meaning. Categorically, though, many of these generalized competencies are applicable to social studies teacher education with some referential and contextual adjustments.

In 1973 the Commission on Multicultural Education and the Committee on Performance-Based Teacher Education of the American Association of Colleges for Teacher Education developed a plan to examine systematically the potential of CBTE for preparing teachers for multicultural school settings. The results of this pioneering effort are published in a document entitled *Multicultural Education Through Competency Based Teacher Education*. The contributing authors discuss competency based multicultural education in general and as it relates to three different ethnic minorities—Blacks, Hispanic Americans, and American Indians. The different ethnic authors have their own unique lists of competencies, but there is some consensus among them, as is evident by the overlap in competencies across authors. A brief summary of some of the authors' viewpoints will serve to illustrate this point, and to indicate the "state of the art" of conceptualizing multicultural teacher education in terms of specified competencies.

Hillard uses a category system for identifying three essential content areas of multicultural teacher education. These are: basic understandings of the cultural relativity and dynamics of the teaching-learning process; skills in cross-cultural communication, diagnosis, analysis, and evaluation of students, learning theories, and instructional methodologies and materials; and positive attitudes that value and promote cultural pluralism.[13] The competencies suggested by Pettigrew for teachers who work specifically in multicultural school settings are primarily of the performance-based type. She gives little attention to knowledge and consequence competencies.[14] The five competency clusters offered by Wynn are rather comprehensive. They encompass understanding human growth and development, planning and preparing for instruction, performing instructional functions, performing achievement functions, displaying pupil achievement, and relating interpersonally.[15] The Community, Home, Cultural Awareness, and Language Training (CHCALT) Model, as described by Mazon and Arciniega, emphasizes four major components: multicultural education philosophy; experience in cultural communities; analytical skill development in language assessment; and diagnostic-prescriptive instructional strategies.[16] Cordova, Jaramillo, and Trujillo's list of competencies include awareness of self and others, the focal points of which are values clarification and knowledge about different ethnic life styles; development of interaction skills in learning environments; assessment of student and teacher behaviors; and organization skills and delivery modes for teaching.[17]

These ideas and others suggested by authors in recent publications with respect to the viability of using a competency based approach to multicultural teacher education are formative and tentative. As such, the competencies listed lack much of the definitiveness and specificity in detail to meet the criteria of CBTE. Many seem more like generic goals than specified competencies. Nevertheless, the efforts of these authors represent a critical first step in an extremely difficult task—interfacing two pedagogical concepts (CBTE and MCE) that, even independently and separately, are plagued by conflicting conceptions with respect to their desirability, viability, and programmatic articulation for improving student achievement and the quality of education. They also are instructive for future attempts at specifying competencies and *systematizing* programs for multicultural teacher education in general, and in particular subject areas.

Multicultural Competencies for Social Studies Teacher Education

Developing a complete list of *specified* competencies for multicultural social studies teacher education is a momentous

PROFESSIONALIZING SOCIAL STUDIES TEACHING

task that far exceeds the limitations of this chapter. Instead, an attempt is made to clarify the three major categorical competencies of the competency based model with respect to multiculturalizing the preparation of social studies teachers. Some examples of the kinds of competencies that might be included in each category are listed. In accordance with the notion that once desired student outcomes—or the kinds of intellectual, social, and emotional growth of students to be achieved—are specified, it becomes easier to determine what teachers need to know and do to effect these changes, consequence competencies are discussed first. These are followed, in sequence, by knowledge and performance competencies.

The competencies for multicultural social studies teacher education discussed below are based upon several major assumptions about the role of teachers in the educational process, general trends in social studies teacher education, and the needs and abilities of students and teachers to comprehend culturally pluralistic content. Some of these assumptions are:

- Teachers are the single most significant variables in the teaching-learning process; the quality of instruction provided to students is primarily a reflection of the quality of the preparation teachers received.
- To date, multicultural education has been conspicuous by its absence in teacher education programs.
- Most teachers, and Americans in general, know very little about ethnic groups other than their own; functionally, they are ethnically illiterate.
- Teachers cannot teach what they do not know; yet, repeatedly, ethnic materials and instructional units have been placed in the hands of untrained or poorly trained social studies teachers with the expectation that they will teach them effectively to students.
- Teachers can be taught to understand cultural and ethnic diversity, and how to do multicultural teaching.
- The anxieties and insecurities many teachers feel toward ethnic students and about teaching ethnically-specific materials stem from a lack of basic knowledge about and experience with different ethnic groups.
- Most Americans live in ethnic enclaves, and few of them have opportunities for sustained contacts and interactions with people outside their own ethnic and social groups.
- Ethnic knowledge is a requisite for full participation in our culturally pluralistic society.
- Cross-cultural participatory and interpersonal interaction

skills are imperatives for effective functionality in our pluralistic society.

These assumptions derive from the philosophical foundations of multicultural education and cultural pluralism. They facilitate the delineation of desired student outcomes and the specification of teachers' knowledge and skills needed to achieve these outcomes.

Consequence Competencies

What are the desired student outcomes of multicultural social studies programs? What will students know and be able to do differently as a result of having experienced multicultural social studies programs? What influences should social studies teachers have on students' attitudes and behaviors relative to ethnic diversity and cultural pluralism? Answers to these questions are, in fact, descriptions of consequence competencies for multicultural social studies teacher preparation programs.

Consequence competencies should be conceived broadly to encompass teacher effectiveness in terms of cognitive, affective, and action student changes. Several examples are presented here to illustrate the array of consequence competencies possible for multicultural social studies education. Programs in social studies teacher education must ensure, among other things, that teachers are successful in facilitating the following student outcomes if they claim to be multicultural and competency based.

- The teacher will increase the capability of students to use multicultural perspectives, interdisciplinary techniques and materials, and situational variables in analyzing ethnic group experiences in the United States.
- The teacher will get students to understand the complexities of the major social, economic, and political problems pervasive in American society, such as limited natural resources, disease, poverty, environmental pollution, and racism, and how these impact upon the lives of different ethnic group members.
- The teacher will improve the moral reasoning ability of students in discussing moral issues and dilemmas with ethnic content.
- The teacher will increase the frequency and effectiveness of the values clarification process employed by students to de-

velop awareness and understanding of their own and others' ethnic and racial values and attitudes.
- The teacher will improve the ability of students to make valid generalizations about ethnic group experiences in America.
- The teacher will succeed in getting students to differentiate by ethnic group between examples and nonexamples of such concepts as culture, socialization, displacement, acculturation, immigration, and desegregation.
- The teacher will get students to demonstrate their understanding of the concepts of inter- and intra-ethnic group similarity and variance through the presentation of specific illustrations, descriptive anecdotes, and demographic data to document their conclusions, observations, and explanations.
- The teacher will succeed in getting students to know themselves better, and to come to grips with their own and others' ethnicity, through the acquisition of more accurate information about one's own and other ethnic groups' histories, cultural traditions, and heritages.
- The teacher will be able to get students to explain and illustrate the meaning of the statement "Many Americans are functional biculturalists, and most Americans are culturally bound in terms of behavior," relative to different ethnic group conceptions of norms, values, preferred behavior, perceptions, and customs.
- The teacher will increase student ability to recognize, describe, and identify negative ethnic stereotypes and alienating communication behaviors, and engage in a deliberate self-growth program aimed at replacing these with accurate information about ethnic groups, positive attitudes, and facilitative language habits to be used with ethnic group members.
- The teacher will get students to demonstrate their pride in self-ethnic identity and cultural heritage by being open and willing to share their own heritages with others, and being receptive and assertive toward learning about other ethnic group experiences.
- The teacher will succeed in getting students to demonstrate their knowledge of ethnic diversity and cultural pluralism in the United States by identifying several different ethnic groups by name and providing both historical and contemporary data about each, such as demographic information, contributions to American culture, national origins, immigration/migration patterns, historical adjustments and adaptations to American conditions, and present status in American society.

- The teacher will improve student ability to communicate and interact with people from different ethnic groups, and within different ethnic settings, without experiencing debilitating fears, hostilities, anxieties, frustrations, and isolation.
- The teacher will improve student effectiveness in using problem-solving techniques to examine ethnically-specific problems and situations, and to solve personal ethnically-based dilemmas.

Knowledge Competencies

What do social studies teachers need to know to teach effectively multicultural content and/or ethnically and culturally different students? What do social studies teachers need to know to achieve the kind of student outcomes suggested above? The competencies listed here in answer to these questions presuppose that teachers are knowledgeable about teaching in general and about the content areas that comprise the social studies, and focus on knowledge needs for multicultural teaching in the social studies.

- Using a multidimensional-multidirectional framework the teacher is able to explain the influences and peoples from internally, north, east, south, and west of the United States that have impacted upon the development of American history, life, and culture.
- The teacher understands the cultural patterns, value systems, and learning styles of different ethnic groups, and how these may affect ethnic students' response patterns in instructional settings.
- The teacher can describe the economic, political, social, and aesthetic contributions of several different ethnic groups, both majority and minority, to American history and culture.
- The teacher can explain the role and impact of different ethnic groups, both majority and minority, in the critical events in America's history, such as colonization, the American Revolution, the Westward expansion, the Vietnamese War, and the civil rights movement, using anthropological, sociological, historical, geographic, and political materials, techniques, and perspectives.
- The teacher understands the communication styles of different ethnic groups.
- The teacher is familiar with a wide variety of content resources and references that present authentic and accurate information about many different dimensions of ethnic life

styles, the concepts of ethnicity and cultural pluralism in general, and methodological resources on teaching multicultural education.
- The teacher is able to identify and explain the major tenets and philosophical concepts of multicultural education and cultural pluralism.
- The teacher understands the concepts of culture and ethnicity in general and in reference to the particular configurations of ethnic groups, experiences, and situations within the context of the American Experience.
- The teacher comprehends the concept of *staging*, or *developmental progression*, as it relates to the ethnic identification process among different ethnic individuals and groups. He or she is able to characterize the stages of ethnic identification suggested by William E. Cross[18] and James A. Banks,[19] apply these stages to analyses of the development of ethnic and cultural consciousness among ethnic groups in the United States, and explain their relevance and implications for interpreting the behavioral patterns of different ethnic students, and for designing relevant culturally pluralistic social studies curriculum consonant with the various stages of ethnic identification.
- The teacher understands that the attitudes and behaviors of ethnically and culturally different students are largely a reflection of their background experiences and cultural conditioning.
- The teacher has a working knowledge of the latest instructional techniques (i.e., inquiry, values analysis, moral dilemmas, simulation, comparative analysis, process conceptualization, etc.) in social studies and multicultural education.
- The teacher is able to describe the social and cultural dynamics operating in multiethnic social studies classrooms.
- The teacher is able to explain the principles of unity and variance within and among ethnic groups in the United States, and how these are potential sources of both cultural conflict and social cohesion and vitality.
- The teacher is able to explain why and how such communication components as vocabulary, nonverbal signs and symbols, preconceptions about communicants, and shared experiential modes or frames of reference can be barriers to cross-cultural communication and inter-ethnic group interactions.
- The teacher can explain and document with specific illustrations the concepts of cultural exchange and adaptation as

they relate to ethnic groups' presence and experiences within, and their impact upon, the American Experience.

These are just a few samples of the kinds of knowledge competencies for inclusion in multicultural social studies teacher education. Many others can be identified. There is no guarantee that the teacher who possesses these knowledge competencies will be able to bring about any or all of the desired changes in student growth. It is true, though, that teachers without them cannot begin to conceptualize and implement sound, comprehensive multicultural instruction in the social studies.

Performance Competencies

As Epstein suggests, "knowledge and sensitivity alone are not enough. The teacher must develop the special skills which enable her to use her knowledge and reflect her sensitivity."[20] Thus, skills, or performance abilities, are a critical component of multicultural competency based social studies teacher education. Performance competencies are derived from the question: What should social studies teachers be able to do to teach multicultural content in the social studies effectively? To answer this question, teacher education programs should include the development of attitudes and behaviors like the ones listed below.

- The teacher is able to develop instructional units (i.e., lessons, themes, courses, etc.) that use multicultural content and multiethnic perspectives to teach social studies concepts, such as immigration and migration, identity, change, power, culture, diversity, and interdependence.
- The teacher is able to develop and use criteria for analyzing and evaluating social studies instructional materials and curriculum designs for their treatment of ethnic group life styles and cultural diversity in American society.
- The teacher has the ability to revise existing social studies instructional materials and curricula to eliminate ethnic biases, overemphases on Anglo-Saxon-centric experiences and perspectives, and to include more culturally pluralistic information and perspectives.
- The teacher can design a variety of student assessment and evaluation criteria and techniques that reflect the cultural experiences of different ethnic groups, and complement their learning styles.

PROFESSIONALIZING SOCIAL STUDIES TEACHING

- The teacher has the ability to use different social studies instructional modes (i.e., inquiry, peer teaching, consensus-based learning activities, values analysis, etc.) that employ multicultural experiences, perspectives, and content.
- The teacher can conceptualize and articulate a personal philosophy of social studies education that is consistent with the tenets of cultural pluralism and can translate this philosophy into program plans and implementation strategies.
- The teacher has the ability to use values clarification techniques and moral dilemma discussions to clarify self and student racial attitudes and values.
- The teacher can apply the pedagogical principles of good teaching to implementing multicultural learning experiences in the social studies, and in working with culturally different students.
- The teacher can use systematic observation orientations and techniques to collect data in different ethnic communities about actual, applied ethnic life styles, and test these findings against theoretical and conceptual constructs of ethnic groups' life styles and cultural characteristics.
- The teacher can demonstrate the ability to use interaction analysis schedules, sociograms, anthropological participant-observer descriptions, and other observation techniques to collect, analyze, and interpret data on the verbal and nonverbal dynamics between students and teachers in ethnically pluralistic social studies classrooms.
- The teacher uses an array of differential questioning strategies to increase ethnic students' participation in class discussions and at different levels of cognitive and intellectual complexity.
- The teacher has respect, positive attitudes, and empathy for students from different cultural backgrounds and ethnic groups.
- The teacher values cultural and ethnic diversity as potentially positive, facilitative forces for improving the quality of life on both personal and societal levels.
- The teacher can differentiate and modulate his or her own communication styles so as to communicate easily and effectively with students from different ethnic groups and cultural backgrounds.

Unfinished Task

Unquestionably, many of the competencies suggested for multicultural competency based programs for social studies teacher education are not restricted to that alone. They are applicable to teacher preparation in general. The competencies described are not an exhaustive list. They are merely illustrative of the kinds of knowledge, skills, and experiences that should be essential components of social studies teacher preparation programs. Nor do they represent "the last word" to be said on the subject. They are still in the embryonic or formative stages of development. They need further refinement and specification as we continue to work toward moving from conceptualizing to implementing programs in multicultural teacher education. It may very well be that levels of specification beyond those described in the preceding pages will evolve from teacher training programs in practice and systematic research on multicultural education.

Despite whatever weaknesses and shortcomings inhere in the competencies discussed in this chapter, they do represent an attempt to bring some more focus and structure to the process of conceptualizing, designing, and implementing training experiences for teacher education students in the areas of multicultural and social studies education. Applying the competency based model to social studies teacher education has the potential of replacing ambiguous experiences, intuitive chance happenings, and speculative results relative to MCE with accountability in the context of well-planned, systematic teacher preparation programs.

Footnotes

[1] Richard H. Hersh, "PBTE and Multi-Cultural Education: If the Shoe Does Not Fit, Should We Wear It?" in *Sifting and Winnowing: An Exploration of the Relationship Between Multi-Cultural Education and CBTE*, Carl A. Grant, ed. (Madison, Wisconsin: Teacher Corps Associates, 1975), pp. 29–45.

[2] James M. Cooper, Howard L. Jones, and Wilford A. Weber, "Specifying Teacher Competencies," *Journal of Teacher Education* 24 (Spring 1973), pp. 17–23.

[3] W. Robert Houston, "Competency Based Education," in *Exploring Competency Based Education*, W. Robert Houston, ed. (Berkeley, California: McCutchan Publishing Corporation, 1974), pp. 3–15.

[4] James A. Banks, *Teaching Strategies for Ethnic Studies* (Boston: Allyn and Bacon, 1975), p. 27.

[5] Geneva Gay, "Organizing and Designing Culturally Pluralistic Curriculum," *Educational Leadership* 33 (December, 1975), p. 178.

[6] James A. Banks, Carlos E. Cortés, Ricardo L. Garcia, Geneva Gay, and Anna S. Ochoa, *Curriculum Guidelines for Multiethnic Education* (Arlington, Virginia: National Council for the Social Studies, 1976), p. 21.

[7] Gwendolyn C. Baker, "Instructional Priorities in a Culturally Pluralistic School," *Educational Leadership* 32 (December, 1974), pp. 176–182.

[8] James A. Banks, "The Implications of Multicultural Education for Teacher Education," in *Pluralism and the American Teacher: Issues and Case Studies*,

Frank H. Klassen and Donna M. Gollnick, eds. (Washington, D.C.: American Association of Colleges for Teacher Education, 1977), pp. 1–30.

[9]John Aragon, "An Impediment to Cultural Pluralism: Culturally Deficient Teachers Attempting to Teach Culturally Different Children," in *Cultural Pluralism in Education: A Mandate for Change*, Madelon D. Strent, William R. Hazard, and Harry N. Rivlin, eds. (New York: Appleton-Century-Crofts, 1973), pp. 77–84.

[10]Jacqueline W. Johnson, "Human Relations Preparation in Teacher Education: The Wisconsin Experience," in *Pluralism and the American Teacher: Issues and Case Studies*, Frank H. Klassen and Donna M. Gollnick, eds. (Washington, D.C.: American Association of Colleges for Teacher Education, 1977), p. 198.

[11]Geneva Gay, "Differential Dyadic Interactions of Black and White Teachers with Black and White Pupils in Recently Desegregated Social Studies Classrooms: A Function of Teacher and Pupil Ethnicity" (Washington, D.C.: National Institute of Education, January, 1974), p. 302.

[12]See, especially, Carl A. Grant, ed., *Sifting and Winnowing: An Exploration of the Relationship Between Multi-Cultural Education and CBTE* and William A. Hunter, ed., *Multicultural Education Through Competency-Based Teacher Education* (Washington, D.C.: American Association of Colleges for Teacher Education, 1974).

[13]Asa G. Hillard, "Restructuring Teacher Education for Multicultural Imperatives," in *Multicultural Education Through Competency-Based Teacher Education*, William A. Hunter, ed. (Washington, D.C.: American Association of Colleges for Teacher Education, 1974), pp. 40–55.

[14]L. Eudora Pettigrew, "Competency-Based Teacher Education: Teacher Training for Multicultural Education," in *Multicultural Education Through Competency-Based Teacher Education*, William A. Hunter, ed., pp. 72–94.

[15]Cordell Wynn, "Teacher Competencies for Cultural Diversity," in *Multicultural Education Through Competency-Based Teacher Education*, William A. Hunter, ed., pp. 95–111.

[16]M. Reyes Mazon and Tomas Arciniega, "Competency-Based Teacher Education and the Culturally Different: A Ray of Hope or More of the Same," in *Multicultural Education Through Competency-Based Teacher Education*, William A. Hunter, ed., pp. 158–173.

[17]Ignacio Cordova, Mari-Luci Jaramillo, and Rupert Trujillo, "Competency-Based Teacher Education for Mexican American Students," in *Multicultural Education Through Competency-Based Teacher Education*, William A. Hunter, ed., pp. 174–193.

[18]William E. Cross, Jr., "The Negro-to-Black Conversion Experience," *Black World* (July, 1971), pp. 13–27.

[19]Banks, "The Implications of Multicultural Education for Teacher Education," pp. 17–26.

[20]Charlotte Epstein, *Intergroup Relations for the Classroom Teacher* (Boston: Houghton Mifflin Company, 1968), p. 50.

7 Competency-Referenced Professional Development

Thomas W. Hewitt

The Professional Dilemma

In a thoughtful study for the American Association of Colleges for Teacher Education, Howsam[1] and others explored the status of education as a profession. The conclusion they reach is that education is not now a profession, but could become so if specific problems related to governance, control of entry, standards for practitioners, and the context of teaching in relation to clients are resolved. This looms as a high order of tasks. It is important to remember, however, that in attaining professional status other occupations have also addressed and resolved similar problems.[2] In that it is feasible to assume teachers can do the same, then teaching constitutes what the report describes as an emergent profession.

It is the contention here that, in the past, inservice education and continuing teacher development have been neglected and that this neglect has impeded the movement toward professional status. As the need for more teachers grew in the period following World War II, preservice concerns became dominant in teacher education. Inservice education was substantially ignored. Today, as the number of needed teachers dwindles, that neglect of inservice education confronts us as one of our major professional dilemmas.

The remedy lies in the reconceptualization of teacher development. As an emergent profession, education must reconsider how it trains and maintains those who serve by teaching. Consideration must be given to how a teacher moves from preservice to inservice and to continuing professional growth. Comprehensive efforts to extend, as well as maintain, the competence of teachers must become a major concern of all who teach, and especially of those who teach teachers.

Historically, there has been no single institution or agency preëminently and consistently concerned with teacher development beyond preservice. Universities and colleges have been involved only where certification and degree purposes were served or when a university consultant service was to be performed. School districts have perennially avoided involvement unless it was thrust upon them. Only recently have teacher organizations begun to exercise claims in this area. To date, professional growth beyond preservice education has been primarily the individual teacher's concern.

Confusion of terms is often associated with thinking about professionalization. Nicholson and Joyce[3] point to the lack of definitional agreement when such terms as staff development, professional development, inservice, teacher renewal, and continuing education are used interchangeably. Such confusion highlights the crucial nature of the problem, for it reflects the failure to structure an image of professional development.

If the failure to think of teaching as a continuous development process is endemic to teaching in general, what of the more specialized aspects of social studies teaching? The answer is the same. There is little in the social studies literature that suggests the condition is any different. With the exception of isolated cases, professional social studies development exists in the content of credential-oriented university and college work, spasmodic job-related inservice efforts, and some organization-related development served by the National Council for the Social Studies or its state and regional affiliates.

In reviewing NCSS yearbooks, special publications, *Social Education*, and other social studies journals, little was found that addressed professional development in the configuration suggested in this chapter. This is not surprising; the advent of this concern is recent.

Despite the lack of thematic treatments among the publications reviewed, some useful articles were found. Most noteworthy is the March 1970 issue of *Social Education*, devoted to "Revitalizing Teacher Education," which contains three articles pertinent to this discussion. A review of the research literature by Joseph C. Grannis[4] provides useful insights on specifics of teaching that are as relevant today as they were then. Jarolimek,[5] Ducharme,[6] and Lowe and Corbin[7] present proposals for inservice training. Collectively, they do not project a professional development thesis, but they do identify what should constitute inservice or graduate study in teacher development after preservice. Most of those proposals would be relevant for teachers today: teaching styles, selecting and using learning resources, individualizing instruction, objectives and evaluations, valuing and decision-making. The major point is that the intent of these articles was to outline suggestions for inservice and further graduate study, not to examine professional development as a comprehensive approach to enhance teaching.

While other articles can be cited in extending this discussion, they would not change the picture that emerges.[8] Overall, there is little to indicate that professionalization in social studies has been more than merely a concern for the traditional views encompassing inservice.

The Idea of Professional Development

Howsam[9] differentiates among types of professional development. The use of the term "inservice" is reserved for activities that arise from the unique needs of a particular workplace, such as the school, as a response to needs within the system of which the workplace is a part. The term "continuing" is used to designate activities that supplement or extend preservice education after a person is certified. Continuing education includes updating on pertinent findings and techniques that are related to an individual's teaching.

Professional development also takes place in a number of different contexts. Delineation of these contexts is important because it provides a framework connecting professional development to the sources from which it arises. The contextual dimensions of professional development are:

- Job-Embedded—development encompassing formal and informal aspects of teaching to include committee work, team teaching, interaction with consultants, professional reading, curriculum analysis.
- Job-Related—development that is not strictly a part of the teacher's job. This context might include workshops, visitations, teacher exchanges, training packages, teacher center activities.
- Credential-Oriented—college-based orientation toward acquiring professional credentials; formal study specific to requirements of degrees or certification.
- Organization-Related—collective teacher actions related to common goals. This can be a general organization such as a union or association; it may also organize around curriculum areas such as social studies.
- Self-Directed—motivation for development intrinsic with the individual teacher. The enablers—time, money, resources—can be provided by schools, higher education institutions, or professional organizations. The forms this may take include

sabbaticals, continuing education, release time, internships.[10]

Each context may serve one or several purposes: general teacher growth; improvement of role competencies; school-related actions that support curricular, instructional implementation as decided within the institution; and/or changes in roles of practitioners. The integration of the professional development types, inservice and continuance, within an appropriate context to serve specific purposes offers a different perspective from which to view the purposes of teacher development and discern new meaning for teacher education. Instead of traditional certification and degree progression, teacher education can be viewed as an integrated process of preservice, inservice, and continuance, supporting the total developmental needs of teachers.

The aim of professional development is to enrich teacher decision-making and the actions that follow so that teaching can achieve an optimal effect. If inservice and continuance, as forms of professional development, are to reflect this purpose, then the elements of teaching—the decisions and actions—must be understood.

Teachers make decisions and take actions consistent with their role perceptions. In part, they are teachers in the sense of decisions and actions that are generalizable to all who teach. These generic teaching behaviors may include decisions and actions about classroom management, administrative procedures, policy implementation, and similar levels of teaching activity. In addition, teachers make specialized decisions and take actions that are unique—that differentiate according to what one teaches. For example, in social studies, the use of chronology, map work, or similar curriculum specific activities requires a special set of decisions and actions that, in content and process, differentiate social studies from other teaching specialties. We speak of this as content specific teaching.

Intervention through decisions and actions occurs in consideration of at least four factors—teaching style, teaching setting or environment, instructional modes, and curriculum content or substance.[11] Each has a content or knowledge base, a performance aspect, and an effect in terms of the teacher-learner interactions. They form an ecological reference for teaching, "... the interaction of all contextual variables ... which produce the performance of both teacher and student. ..."[12] The ecology of teaching concerns the fit of the dimensions of teaching with participants. It constitutes an emergent theoretical structure important for the non-linear perspective it provides in viewing teaching and learning as a set of new dynamics. Dreeben,[13] Lortie,[14] and Barker,[15] among others, point out that the theory and research base developed to date does not provide a satisfactory framework for knowing what goes on when teaching occurs. The ecological perspective allows teaching to be viewed as a complex, polymorphic phenomenon, the understanding of which allows the reinterpretation of performance and effects.

Continuity and change are important aspects in the professional development process. Continuity between what one acquires in preservice and continuing practice requires *maintenance* of competencies over time. On the other hand, as one teaches and acquires experience and knowledge, some of what was known may change. A competency or set of competencies may be altered, modified, discarded, or assimilated into a new competency or set that was not known or performed at the time of preservice. This *transformational* quality is also important. Both *maintenance* and *transformation* should be served through professional development.

Reconstructing the Professional Approach

Professional development is a characteristic of professional status. The evidence suggests that as a recognized activity in teaching, it does not exist. It is suggested here that a reconceptualization of professional development is needed. Distinctions should be made between inservice and continuing education. Inservice should be viewed as job-related competency development based on institutional needs. Continuance should address the maintenance and transformational needs of teachers as they mature and become more distant from their preservice experience. Emphasis in professional development should be placed on the refinement and/or acquisition of teaching competencies. A competency based professional development construct is proposed here which attempts to integrate the maintenance-transformation function with the decisions-actions configuration and ecological perspective mentioned earlier.

Maintenance-Transformation

Social studies teachers receive preservice work in intellectual development (questioning, conceptual development, generalizing, etc.), inquiry modes, technical skills such as working with maps, and numerous other content-process elements. The classroom experience provides practice for keeping these in use. However, inservice support must be emplaced if the full range of preservice learning is to be maintained. At the same time, changes in practice, new knowledge, even new techniques occur to which the teacher often does not have access. Continuance as a type of professional development is critical to transforming teaching competencies so that the social studies teacher can be enhanced by what has changed since the original training period. Current practice suggests that opportunities for teachers to maintain and transform their competencies may occur through workshops, reading journals, attending conferences, or accidentally finding out from someone else. This is at best a haphazard process. Professional development should ensure that such opportunities are planned, rather than piecemeal, events.

Decisions-Actions

Professional development must be in accord with the nature of the teacher-learner interaction which is essentially a practitioner-client relationship. The substance of the relationship is the decision-action pattern that the teacher utilizes in relation to the learning setting and the learner.[16] Keeping in mind that this is influenced by factors such as the classroom as an environment, the school or workplace as a complex of related factors, the service provided is one of continuous decisions that prompt actions to move the learner in a hoped-for direction toward learning.

The decision-action concept is not only the substance of teaching, it is also the substance of professional development. Improvement in making the best decision from a number of possibilities and in turn taking the best action from a number of possibilities is necessary to enhance teaching. The preservice period is the beginning of applied knowledge through deciding and acting. As a first level, it is complete only in the limited experiences that permit it to occur. As years pass and teaching experiences multiply, the decision-action process becomes refined in that passage. It is imperative to teacher growth that the limited initial basis for the decision-action configuration be expanded by an opportunity to study it, to determine what facets should be maintained and what transformations occur or are needed. We do not know what support mechanisms, such as clinical training, can be or would be of use. The social studies teacher's decision-action process may be altered by what social studies teaches, but how do we focus on ways to improve what is taught? The decisions made, the actions taken as a teacher in general and in teaching social studies, must be a focus of professional development.

Ecological Concept

The actions and decisions of social studies teachers occur amid complex factors. These factors can be placed in at least four contexts which reflect the physical aspects and subtle atmosphere of the classroom.[17] Physical aspects suggest those decisions-actions about classroom arrangements, how furniture is selected, where it is placed, spacing, and the form physical facilities take. The physical aspect also suggests perceptual conditions. Uses of color, decoration, fabrics, and other items can affect human interaction in a range from warm to cold and open to closed. Under what physical-atmospheric conditions is social studies best taught? Does it vary with the personal perceptual styles of individuals? Does the setting-as-environment configuration enhance the decision-action interplay? These are but a few of the aspects of setting that can affect the teaching of social studies. Much of what is known is new. It may not have been a preservice concern. But if the social studies is to be taught at an optimum level, competence in knowing how to physically and atmospherically prepare a classroom is of importance.

A second dimension—style—references the individual teacher's and learner's way of presenting themselves. The teacher's personality, learning manner, dress, habits, and behaviors create an image. Are they open or closed? Do teachers inadvertently select children and youth for more positive, or negative, attention? If a teacher presents a specific teaching style, to what extent do children and youth differ in how they relate to that style or alternate ones? If differences do occur, do they reflect variances between personal styles—or is learning also a set of styles in addition to personal styles? Styles can be viewed as complex presentations of the person. They are critical aspects of individual behavior that affect the teacher-learner interaction. Professional development should promote teachers' awareness of personal and teaching styles.

The instructional strategies and/or materials a teacher uses are also important. Studies indicate that teachers, like their students, attend to learning in different ways and with differing intensity if various instructional techniques and technology are used.[18] In social studies, with a wealth of instructional materials and technology at hand, how does the use of maps, globes, simulation, games, and other instructional devices enhance or inhibit learning? If instruction by the teacher is to promote learning, instruction as the delivery system assumes a greater importance in professional growth.

The curriculum is a fourth factor. Decisions about selection of materials, content sequences, and the ordering of information issue from what is known about what is learned. The degree to which a curriculum is simple, abstract, visual, multisensory, static, or dynamic patterns a learner's attending to it. Teachers vary in how they make curriculum. Is it necessary to have a uniform curriculum or should it be individualized consistent with learner characteristics? These aspects of curriculum and the decisions made about them suggest that teachers have much to consider about a part of teaching that has often seemed rather a mundane concern.

These factors—contextual setting, instruction, style, and curriculum—interrelate and are embedded in any teaching decision. Ecologically they form a perspective about the nature of teaching that gives decisions and actions a comprehensive, holistic quality. These are perhaps minimum reference points for a professional design. In this sense, they serve as both the subject for attention in teaching and as the conditions for attending to the process of professional development.

Competency Construct

The final consideration in this construct for professional development in teaching addresses the competencies to be acquired. The linkage among other components in professional development is the range of competencies obtained in preservice beginnings which are maintained and transformed throughout a teaching career. Competencies refer to those skills, knowledges, attitudes, and behaviors that teachers deploy consistently and continually in teaching. Whether they are generic, as in establishing instructional set or organizing the classroom, and common to all teachers, or whether they are special, as in discrete skills attributable only to use in social studies (map, globe skills, for example), they represent the personal set of actions that teachers utilize. By focusing on clarifying the knowledge, performance, and consequence aspects of various teaching behaviors, the competency based approach helps to define and establish the specifics of what teachers do when they teach. Whether one adheres to a purist or less confining view of competency based education may not be as important as whether one references the practice of social studies teaching in the mind set that competency-referencing requires. It is not so much the precision of talking about competence as it is the framing of what we do as competencies specific to criteria for their demonstration. Herein lies the worth of competency based education. It affords us a framework for linking and monitoring what is acquired in preservice with what is maintained as practitioners. It provides us with an itinerary for our professional journey.

The four conceptual structures form a construct suggesting considerations useful in thinking about professional development. The cautious use of a construct rather than the articulation of a theory or model is intentional. It provides a means to establish the idea of professional development. From it, several ideas can be projected that suggest some further lines of thought.

Implications of Competency-Referenced Professional Development

Professional development depends in part on knowing what teachers and teacher trainers think are the needs in teaching social studies. The problem is not in getting the information. Information can and should be obtained from a number of different sources. The problem is establishing why the information is needed and how it can be of use. Information gathering must be an inclusive part of a broader strategy to establish the base for productive professional growth. If instructional needs are identified, an inservice strategy may serve that purpose. If individual teacher needs are the concern, a strategy for continuance may be in order. The primary concern should be to evolve a strategy characterized by continuity over time, a continuous support system, consistent with the type of professional growth needed.

In devising a strategy, needs are often translated into broad areas of teaching such as curriculum development, instructional processes, or modes of evaluation. Such an approach often merely transmits information *about* teaching; transformation of teaching behaviors is left to chance. Another line of thought suggests that a competency-referencing strategy may be appropriate. One such strategy, based on a competency based teacher education program, followed teachers from preservice through the first year and a half of teaching.[19] Working from their preservice competency structure, teachers in the initial teaching experience provided an information base for identifying specific competency-referenced needs. These needs were projected as a basis for possible professional development activities through inservice and individualized professional development. In this situation, the competency-referencing strategy provided a basis for continuity in professional growth and a more precise means to support development of identified needs. Efforts like this, however modest, need to be considered if any systematic basis for professional development is to emerge.

Inservice must be one part of a comprehensive professional plan. Presently, it is often tied to the certification and degree process, a form of professionalization through schooling to the highest degree. Perhaps consideration of a non-traditional approach to certification and graduate level work is required. The emphasis for study, certification, and degree attainment in a professional context must be one of fitting these to the person in the workplace, not one of fitting the person to requirements outside it. The competency-referenced construct offers a linking mechanism through which study, certification, and degree attainment can be based on the practitioner in the workplace. The role of higher education becomes that of serving teachers through their teaching needs. This type of integrating experience has been successfully used in a variety of settings by Teacher Corps projects.

The emphasis in focusing on an inservice-continuance process of professional development is to point at the need for creating a new generation of models and theories as the basis for the study of professional development. David Hunt's[20] matching-models concept, the *Models of Teaching* developed by Joyce,[21] and the five-volume Inservice Teacher Education study[22] provide a new resource base for devising needed models and theories. Perhaps it would be fruitful to review again the various models on preservice,[23] and re-think them in light of professional development needs. The point is: there is a repository of information that could be useful if we redirect our attention and view things in new ways.

Attention should also be turned to the use of the professional development construct to focus on the purposes of social studies in schools. The social studies curriculum evolved in part as a response to shifting public views on what purpose schooling in social studies should serve. The need to reflect continually on purpose is critical to any proposal for professional development. What content and skill emphasis will prevail? This is problematic to the passage of time and changes in public attitudes on education. As purposes of social studies shift, teachers of social studies must accommodate to those changes. This means that concerns for acquiring new information and new techniques must become part of the individual's professional development through inservice and continuance. This suggests that through those concerns the purpose of having social studies as part of the schooling process, the rationale for social studies, will become a focus for both program attainment and professional growth. Practice and purpose thus become inseparable—forming a foundation for social studies teaching and professional development.

A final implication reflects the concern over how and by whom control of professional development shall be exercised. The professional development construct postulates a mutual concern for inservice and continuance. The construct emphasizes a need for collaborative behavior in deciding how professional growth shall occur and toward what certification, degree ends, or personal growth objectives it shall move. Professional status, if it is to be achieved, requires agreement by all parties in resolving how control will be exercised. Professionals must control their profession. If teachers are to be professionals, then they must be the source for determining how control is exercised on their behalf.

Conclusion

Traditional views and practices concerning the professional development of teachers prevail. Contemporary needs demand a different approach to teacher growth; a process of professional development extending from preservice training to career termination. The concepts of inservice and continuance have been offered as a reference for reconceptualizing teacher growth in a professional context. The professional development construct discussed sought to provide a framework in which a new emphasis on competency-referenced professional development could be worked out. At various points, the implications for the teacher of social studies have been discussed. It is important to emphasize that all of these ideas are proposed as a beginning, a hesitant start to redress our professional dilemma. The necessary transformation is seen in outline. Professionals must look beyond what exists toward what could be—a profession confirmed in its maturity through a process of continuous professional development.

Footnotes

[1] Robert B. Howsam, Dean C. Corrigan, George W. Denmark, and Robert J. Nash, *Educating a Profession* (Washington, D.C.: American Association of Colleges for Teacher Education, 1976). This work will hereafter be referenced as the Howsam Report.

[2] Medicine, for example, has not always been associated with a professional concept. Professional status enjoyed by medicine today owes much to the comprehensive, long-term development that commenced after publication of Abraham Flexner's *Medical Education in the United States and Canada*. (Boston: D. B. Updike, The Merrymont Press, 1910).

[3] Alexander M. Nicholson and Bruce R. Joyce, *ISTE Report III, Literature on Inservice Teacher Education: An Analytic Review* (Palo Alto, California: Inservice Teacher Education Concept Project sponsored by the National Center for Education Statistics and Teacher Corps, 1976), pp. 79–90.

[4] Joseph C. Grannis, "The Social Studies Teacher and Research on Teacher Education," *Social Education* 34 (March 1970), pp. 291–301, p. 315.

[5] John Jarolimek, "A Model for Inservice Teachers," *Social Education* 34 (March 1970), pp. 329–332.

[6] Raymond A. Ducharme, "Neglected Resources for Teacher Training," *Social Education* 34 (March 1970), pp. 318–323.

[7] William T. Lowe and Warren Corbin, "Learning to Teach the Social Studies: What Do Teachers Recommend?" *Social Education* 34 (March 1970), pp. 286–290, p. 352.

[8] For example, see John D. Haas, "Diffusion of Curriculum Products Through Inservice Education" (Paper presented at the annual meeting of the National Council for the Social Studies, 1974); Madison Public Schools, *Development of an Inservice Model for Implementing New Methodology in the Social Studies Curriculum* (Madison, Wisconsin: Madison Public Schools, 1970); Jack Sutherland, "Revitalizing the Teacher—A Political View," *Social Studies Review* 15 (September 1976), pp. 19–23.

[9] Howsam Report, pp. 65–66.

[10] Nicholson and Joyce, *ISTE Report III*, pp. 6–16.

[11] Thomas W. Hewitt, "Conceptualization of a Decision Process for Use in Social Studies Teacher Education" (Unpublished doctoral dissertation, University of Houston, 1971).

[12] William J. Tikunoff, Beatrice A. Ward, and Franklin D. Stacy, "Toward Ecologically-Based Curriculum: A Model for Professional Growth Through Participatory Research and Development" (An invited paper presented at the annual meeting of the Association of Teacher Educators, Atlanta, Georgia, February 1977), p. 4.

[13] Robert Dreeben, "Good Intentions," *School Review* 83 (November 1974), pp. 37–47.

[14] Dan C. Lortie, *Schoolteacher: A Sociological Study* (Chicago: University of Chicago Press, 1975).

[15] Robert G. Barker, *Ecological Psychology: Concepts and Methods for Studying the Environments of Human Behavior* (Stanford, California: Stanford University Press, 1968).

[16] The conceptions projected here are mine. For additional information, see Alvin I. Goldman, *A Theory of Human Action* (Englewood Cliffs, New Jersey: Prentice-Hall, 1970); Frank A. Schmidtlein, "Decision Process Paradigms in Education," *Educational Researcher* 4 (May 1974), pp. 4–11.

[17] See the special issue "Learning Environments," *School Review* 82 (August 1974) and Robert Sommer's *Design Awareness* (New York: Holt, Rinehart and

Winston, 1972), or his earlier work, *Personal Space* (Englewood Cliffs, New Jersey: Prentice-Hall, Inc., 1969).

[18]This is one finding among several in a report by Gordon Lawrence and others dealing with teachers and inservice for the State of Florida. See Gordon Lawrence, et al., "Patterns of Effective Inservice Education," *Inservice* (February 1977), pp. 1–3, p. 8. This publication is a newsletter of the National Council of States on Inservice Education.

[19]Thomas W. Hewitt, "Using Social Studies CBTE as a Basis for Inservice Design," (Manuscript in process), 1977.

[20]David E. Hunt, *Matching Models in Education* (Toronto, Canada: Ontario Institute for Studies in Education, 1971).

[21]Bruce R. Joyce and Marsha Weil, *Models of Teaching* (Englewood Cliffs, New Jersey: Prentice-Hall, Inc., 1972).

[22]Inservice Teacher Education Concepts Project sponsored by the National Center for Education Statistics and the Teacher Corps. The study produced five reports published in 1976–1977: *Report I, Issues to Face; Report II, Interviews: Perceptions of Professionals and Policy Makers; Report III, The Literature on Inservice Teacher Education: An Analytic Review; Report IV, Creative Authority and Collaboration; Report V, Cultural Pluralism and Social Change*. These reports are available from the National Dissemination Center, Syracuse University, School of Education, Syracuse, New York 13210.

[23]I have reference here to John R. Verduin, Jr., *Conceptual Models in Teacher Education* (Washington, D.C.: American Association of Colleges for Teacher Education, 1967) and the various models on elementary education that were developed in the 1960s.

Index

Names

Airasian, Peter, 50, 54
Aragon, John, 90
Arciniega, Tomas, 92
Arnold, Daniel S., 53

Baker, Gwendolyn C., 90
Banks, James A., 89, 90, 97
Barker, Robert G., 106
Benedict, Ruth, 29
Berliner, David C., 50
Beyer, Barry, 77
Bloom, Benjamin, 42, 87
Bruner, Jerome S., 19, 33

Cooper, James H., 46, 50, 86
Corbin, Warren, 103
Cordova, Ignacio, 92
Cross, William E., 97

Dewey, John, 18, 24, 33-34
Dodl, Norman R., 47
Dodson, Dan W., 27
Dreeben, Robert, 106
Ducharme, Raymond A., 103

Elam, Stanley, 41, 44-45, 82

Fenton, Edwin, 75

Gay, Geneva, 71-72, 89, 91
Goldstein, Jane McCarthy, 71
Grannis, Joseph C., 103

Hall, Gene E., 42, 50, 82
Harmin, Merrill, 75-76
Hersh, Richard H., 86
Hewitt, Thomas W., 72
Hillard, Asa G., 91-92
Hollis, Loye Y., 39
Houston, W. Robert, 44, 45, 86
Howsam, Robert B., vii-viii, 1, 44, 45, 102, 104
Hunt, David, 111
Hunt, Maurice P., 75

Jaramillo, Mari-Luci, 92
Jarolimek, John, 2, 76, 103
Jefferson, Thomas, 35
Johnson, Jacqueline W., 90

Jones, Howard L., 42, 46, 50, 82, 86
Joyce, Bruce R., 103, 111

Kay, Patricia M., 52
Kohlberg, Lawrence, 76, 77

Lortie, Dan C., 106
Lowe, William T., 103
Lyke, Robert F., 27

Massanari, Karl, 52, 55
Mazon, M. Reyes, 92
McLuhan, Marshall, 7
Merrow, John G. G., II, 53
Metcalf, Lawrence E., 75
Morine, Greta, 50

Nicholson, Alexander M., 103

Parsons, James B., 78
Pettigrew, L. Eudora, 92

Rathbone, Charles, 82
Raths, Louis E., 75-76
Remy, Richard C., 23
Roth, Robert A., 52-53

Schomburg, Carl E., 39
Simon, Sidney B., 75-76
Spencer, Herbert, 19
Steffenson, James, 43, 44
Sweeney, Jo Ann Cutler, 78

Toffler, Alvin, 41
Trujillo, Rupert, 92

Ward, Beatrice, 50
Weber, Wilford A., 46, 50, 71, 82, 86
Wynn, Cordell, 92

Subject-Matter

AACTE, 102; Bicentennial Commission, 11, 12, 77-78; PBTE project, 44, 54, 91; Commission on Multicultural Education, 91.
Academic freedom, 10, 15.
Accountability, 1, 54, 86; learner, 3, 45, 46, 52; teacher, 9, 54, 89; student, 59, 60, 81, 82.
Accreditation. *See* Certification.
Adaptability, human, 21-23.
Affective education, and CBTE, 71, 73-84.
Affective student outcomes, 74, 76, 87.

Affective teaching competencies, 48, 49, 62, 74, 76–80, 86.
Aptitude, redefined, 42, 44.
Assessment: criteria for, 2, 5–6, 45, 59, 60; of student competency, 34, 45, 50, 52, 67; procedures, 45, 51, 59; guidelines, examples of, 67–68.
Assumptions, as hypotheses reflecting value judgments, 46, 58, 62–63.

Basics, of education, 17–20; of social studies, 17, 20–33, 35; of CBTE, 85–86.
Bureau of Educational Personnel Development Task Force '72, 43.

Certification, standards for, vi, viii, 12, 20, 34; PBTC, 53.
Change. *See* Continuity.
Citizenship Education, 18, 20, 23–24, 71, 75.
Cognitive competencies, 8, 48, 74, 88.
Community, Home, Cultural Awareness, and Language Training Model, 92.
CBTE, role of, 5–6; definition and description, 44–52; present status and future prospects, 52–55.
CBTE model, testing of, 67–69.
Competencies, defined, viii, 45, 46, 58; fundamental, 17–20; as hypotheses, 55, 58–59; demonstrated, 60, 81.
Competency construct, 109–110.
Competency-referenced professional development, 102–114.
Consequence competencies, 48, 49, 86, 88, 92, 94–96, 109.
Consequence and evaluation, 64, 66–67. *See also*, Assessment.
Content selection, 33, 78.
Continuity, and change, 7, 44, 106; societal, 31–32, 33; schools' commitment to, 31; as strategy, 110, 112.
Criteria and procedures, public, 2, 81.
Criterion referenced assessment, viii, 6, 50.
Culture, preservation of. *See* Continuity.
Curriculum content, 1, 2, 3, 109.
Curriculum Guidelines for Multi-ethnic Education, 89, 90.

Decision-action pattern, 107–108.
Decision-making, 27–28, 105; student, 32, 61, 88, 103; rational, 63, 64, 68.
Demonstration of competencies. *See* Accountability, student.
Developments in social & behavioral sciences, 41, 42.

Ecological concept of teaching, 105–106, 108–109.
Educating a Profession, 76–77, 82.
Elementary Models Project, 4–5, 43.
Elementary Teacher Education, 43.
EPDA, 5.
Evaluation. *See*, Assessment.
Events literacy, 13, 23, 30.
Exploratory competencies, 48, 86–87.

Federal government, increased involvement in education, 41, 43–44.
Flexibility, 74, 82.
Field-centered programs, 51–52.

Generic competencies, 12, 13, 59, 60.
Generic teaching competencies, 61, 105, 109–110.
Goals: as definition of social studies, 12–14; lack of consensus on, 19–20; educational, 35, 40; distinguished from competencies, 48; statements of, examples, 63–64; determination of, 64–65.

History of CBTE, 40–44, 102.

Implementation and demonstration, 64, 65–66.
Individualized instruction, 46, 51, 59, 82; problem of, 42, 45, 103.
Inquiry, 3, 107; rational, 29, 63, 64; strategy, 48, 87; skills, 66, 68.
Inservice education, 12, 13, 55, 89, 102–114. *See also*, Preservice education, Teacher education.
Inservice Teacher Education, 111.
Institute for Responsive Education, 10.
Instructional design, 50, 64, 65.
Instructional modules, 50–51, 59.
Instructional objectives, 48; chart, 49.
Instructional systems approach, 59, 74, 80–82.
Instructional techniques, 87, 108–109.
Intervention, vii, 105–106.

Knowledge competencies, 45, 49; for

teachers, 8, 13, 45, 62, 77–78, 80–81, 86, 87, 92, 96–98, 109. *See also*, Cognitive competencies.

Learning styles, 61, 108.

Mainstream culture, 21–22.
Maintenance of competencies, 106–107. *See also*, Inservice education.
Mastery learning, 42, 43, 44, 87.
Maturation of education profession, 41, 42–43. *See also*, Professionalization.
Models of Teaching, 111.
Models Project, 43, 44.
Moral education, in classroom, 8, 77, 94; moral development, 63, 64, 75, 76.
Multicultural competencies, 92–99.
Multicultural education, 13, 41, 63, 64; and CBTE, 71–72, 83–101.
Multicultural Education Through Competency Based Teacher Education, 91.
Multi-State Consortium of Performance Based Teacher Education, 43.

National Center for Improvement of Educational Systems, 44.

NCSS, 10, 89, 90, 103.
National Science Foundation, 5, 43.

Performance competencies, vi, vii, 49, 88; for teachers, 13, 45–50, 62, 77–78, 80–81, 86, 87, 98–99, 109.
Precision and flexibility, 81, 82.
Preservice education, 12, 35, 62–67, 89. *See also*, Inservice education, Teacher education.
Preservice programs, 15, 54, 55, 72, 89.
Preservice teacher, 60, 67.
Primary institutions, 6–9, 22, 34–35.
Professionalization, & CBTE, vi–ix, 39, 102, 111; problems with, 1, 9–12; development of, 4–5, 15, 72.
Program design, 74, 78, 81; expectations, examples of, 78–80.
Program planning in teacher education, 72, 86.
Professional approach, 13, 106–110.
Professional culture, 11, 15.
Professional development, 102, 104–106.

Research and Development Centers, 43.
Research and development, 41, 43, 55.
Right to learn, 1, 4, 8, 14, 15, 42; right

HOW TO ORDER

This book has been sent free to Comprehensive Members of the National Council for the Social Studies. Information about ordering is as follows:

Title: **Competency Based Teacher Education: Professionalizing Social Studies Teaching**

Editor: **Dell Felder**   Price: **$5.95** Stock No. **498-15270**

When ordering, specify title, editor, price, and stock number. *Payment must accompany all orders except those on official institutional order forms.* No orders can be billed for less than $5.00. Terms: 30 days net; no cash discount. Prices quoted are net, effective May 5, 1978, f.o.b. Waldorf, Maryland, and are subject to change without notice.

Shipping and handling charges will be added to all billed purchase orders. NCSS pays postage and handling on all cash orders. Orders are shipped in the most economical way for normal delivery. *If materials are needed to meet a specific deadline, indicate date required and authorize additional shipping charges.*

Discounts: 10–49 copies, 10%; 50–99 copies, 15%; 100 or more copies, 20%. On purchases made for resale (bookstores, shipped to one address), 20% discount regardless of quantity ordered.

(See reverse side for order form.)

to teach, 1, 3, 4, 10, 13, 15.
Role of teachers, 93–94.

School, as institution, 6–9, 72.
School Based Teacher Educators, 52, 62, 66, 68.
Secondary institutions, 6–9, 14–15.
Social Education, 103.
Socialization, 21, 35.
Society: participation in, 1–2, 32, 68; goals of, 5; shared values of, 23–25, 32; interaction in, 25–27, 32; sanctions for control of, 25–26, 28–30, 33.
Specialized competencies, 13, 59, 109–110.
Student outcomes, 74–76.
Sunshine Laws, 27–28.

Task Force to Study Programs Leading to Certification for Teachers of Social Studies, The, 77.

Teacher competencies, 46, 47, 73, 74.
Teacher Corps, 5, 43, 44, 54, 111.
Teacher education, 4–5, 12–16, 33–36, 93–94. *See also*, Inservice education, Preservice education.
Teacher effectiveness. *See*, Consequence competencies.
Teaching styles, 108.
Technological advances, 41–42.
Training Teachers of Teachers, 5, 43, 44.
Transformation of competencies, 106–107.

University of Houston CBTE Model, 39, 58–62.
U.S. Office of Education, 43, 44.

Values clarification, 63, 64, 68, 75–76, 87, 94–95.
Values education, 23–25.

Index prepared by Mary W. Matthews
Typography by Byrd PrePress
Printing and binding by Waverly Press
Book design and production by Joseph Perez
Cover photo by Algimantas Kezys, S.J.

ORDER FORM

Send completed order plus payment to:

National Council for the Social Studies, Publications Sales,
2030 M Street, N.W. Suite 400, Washington, D.C. 20036.

Title: **Competency Based Teacher Education: Professionalizing Social Studies Teaching**

Editor: **Dell Felder** Stock No. **498-15270**

Quantity _____Price: **$5.95** Total _____

Ship order to:

Name: _____

Address:_____

City:_____ State: _____ Zip No. _____

(See other side for ordering information)